PEIRCE'S EPISTEMOLOGY

PEIRCE'S EPISTEMOLOGY

by

WILLIAM H. DAVIS

Auburn University

MARTINUS NIJHOFF / THE HAGUE / 1972

ISBN 90 247 1296 3

PRINTED IN THE NETHERLANDS

CONTENTS

PREFACE

This work is an essay in Peirce's epistemology, with about an equal emphasis on the "epistemology" as on the "Peirce's." In other words our intention has not been to write exclusively a piece of Peirce scholarship—hence, the reader will find no elaborate tying in of Peirce's epistemology to other portions of his thought, no great emphasis on the chronology of his thought, etc. Peirce scholarship is a painstaking business. His mind was labyrinthine, his terminology intricate, and his writings are, as he himself confessed, "a snarl of twine." This book rather is intended perhaps even primarily as an essay in epistemology, taking Peirce's as the focal point. The book thus addresses a general philosophical audience and bears as much on the wider issue as on the man. I hope therefore that readers will give their critical attention to the problem of knowledge and the suggestions we have developed around that problem and will not look here in the hope of finding an exhaustive piece of Peirce scholarship.

The problem of knowledge is fundamental, exciting, and of course difficult in the extreme. But Peirce's contribution to our thinking on this subject has been of the first magnitude, both in its substance and in its seminal power. Anyone interested in the philosophy of science, the philosophy of religion, logic, or any other field where the nature and validity of human knowledge are central issues can not help but profit from an exposure to Peirce's original and marvelously incisive examination of the life of the mind. I have never read a philosopher who thought otherwise. The reader may be sure that any time he spends with Peirce, even at second remove as in the case of this book, will splendidly widen his intellectual horizons. And I naturally hope that my own rethinking of the issues involved will not dilute but will rather to some modest degree enrich this essay.

To My Parents

INTRODUCTION

Peirce is a man who has diligently and seriously concerned himself with the major traditional problems of philosophy. Peirce makes an honest effort to examine and to solve them to the best of his ability. His effort to solve some of the great classical problems always has *this* merit: it is honest, forthright, manly, sober and intelligent. One does not have to agree with his conclusions in any given case or in any case at all to be able to recognize the professional spirit in Peirce. He is not a poet; he is not a scoffer; he is not trifling with his readers or with the great issues with which he deals. He is not a pedant or a "scholar" of the unoriginal type who plays with footnotes and toys with subtle interpretations of obscure issues or philosophers. He is not playing games. Rather he is attacking the real problems which have concerned and bothered thoughtful people since the days of Thales.

If one were forced to pick out *one* philosophical problem and call that one problem the *major* problem of philosophy, I would want to suggest that that issue would be the one called *scepticism*. In some sense the major battle has not been so much between *this* view of reality and *that* view of reality as it has been between those who believe that, whatever reality is, it can be known by men, and those who believe that it cannot be. Plato, who, by anybody's reckoning must be placed among the giants of the history of ideas for the thoroughness with which he both raised and discussed virtually all the major issues, had at bottom an anti-sceptical motivation. Aristotle and the Christian philosophers dealt profoundly with the problems of scepticism too, but Descartes was the one who brought the problem of scepticism to the fore in a really dramatic way so that in a real and important sense he can rightly be called the father of modern pholosophy. I will not elaborate further on this theme for it would be a long story to trace the role of scepticism in the thought of the classical philosophers of the Continent and of England, and in modern times the place of scepticism in existentialism and positivism (both of which schools have, in their own way, embraced the doctrine to a large degree.)

One could probably view the history of philosophy from some other vantage point which would be as interesting and as valid as the one I have suggested. But if one is willing to allow some merit to the point of view I have outlined – and the only merit I am claiming for it is that it is a suggestive way of hanging the whole thing together – then one will have to allow that the central problem of philosophy is logical or epistemological: what is *reasoning*, what is *knowledge*, and how can they be *justified?* Peirce is mainly noted for what he said on the subject of pragmatism, but I believe that the importance the world has attached to that phase of his thought is partly a matter of historical accident – that is, the scholars hit upon a subject of much interest at a particular stage in the development of American thought. For myself, on the other hand, I believe Peirce's greatness lies in his sustained attack upon the intractable problem of knowledge.

Peirce's doctrine of abduction or retroduction is perhaps as great a philosophical insight as any which has ever been made. Peirce says that the doctrine of the association of ideas was among the greatest of philosophical insights, and is it not probable that the notion of abduction is at least as great as that? In fact, the doctrine of abduction subsumes the doctrine of association under itself as a special case in the way Einstein's theories do Newton's.

Peirce never failed to be stimulating and creative, and his more purely metaphysical theories – particularly his doctrine of categories – have these considerable merits. But somehow it seems easier to be sceptical and critical of these aspects of his thought than of his discussion on the nature of reasoning and thinking. Certainly I have not made it a secret in the following pages that I approve of metaphysics in principle, and Peirce's system is perhaps as good as any that has ever been suggested. Still, his system seems very speculative indeed, and we may well sympathize with Peirce's critics who show a marked coolness toward some of Peirce's more Hegelian utterances. But Peirce's long study of logic and his first-hand acquaintance with the scientific method seem to me to have paid off handsomely in his doctrine of abduction – its creative nature, its fallible nature, its self-corrective nature, its tendency toward the truth, its justification of common-sense, its relation to deduction and induction as the most basic thought process. I do not find most students of Peirce seeing the importance, the truly revolutionary importance, of the doctrine of abduction that I see, and I would like to cause some change in emphasis in this direction. I believe I have Peirce on my side in this, as he seems to give ample hints that he viewed abduction and its consequences and implications as at the heart of what he had to offer the philosophical world.

This present work takes as its particular theme Peirce's assertion (5.348) [1] that the problem of how synthetic reasoning is possible is the "*lock on the door of philosophy.*" Peirce means this quite literally. The first step in understanding Peirce's treatment of this central philosophical question is to examine some of the central positions of Cartesianism. Descartes is rightly called the father of modern philosophy, and for Peirce he is the father of modern philosophy's chief errors. The central assumptions of Descartes' system are, for Peirce, most pernicious errors and have disastrous consequences. To put the whole matter briefly, the foundation of Descartes' system consists in the belief that all knowledge is based upon primitive intuitions. Peirce's alternative to this is that knowledge is a process of flowing inferences.

Peirce divides synthetic reasoning into two divisions, inductive and abductive. The latter, original with him, is understood as the hypothesis-building process. Our second chapter is concerned with examining this form of reasoning. In that chapter we also try to shed some light on the longstanding problem in Peirce interpretation concerning his pragmatic criterion for the exclusion of meaningless hypotheses. We argue that his pragmatic maxim was always meant by him to be interpreted in a very wide sense and never in a positivistic sense. One of the few times Peirce ever admitted making a mistake is when he confesses that he was in error in stating once that his pragmatic maxim was too nominalistic. His mistake was in thinking that he had made a mistake. When interpreted rightly, i.e., broadly enough, the maxim is neither nominalistic nor positivistic.

The third chapter is an elaboration of Peirce's statement that "*approximation must be the fabric out of which our philosophy has to be built.*" (1.404) Paradoxically, the admission that all ampliative (synthetic) reasoning is fallible, instead of leading one into a sceptical position, points the only way out of scepticism. In this section two other thoughts are developed: (1) Knowledge is a self-corrective process; (2) Knowledge grows organically and not from primitive axioms.

The fourth chapter examines the role of instinct in the abductive pro-

---

[1] Charles Sanders Peirce, *Collected Papers of Charles Sanders Peirce,* edd., Charles Hartshorne and Paul Weiss (Cambridge: The Belknap Press of Harvard University Press, 1960). Citations in the text will be to this work and will follow the standard form: the first number indicating the volume, and the second the paragraph.

cess. The fifth chapter concludes with some general reflections upon the wider implications of Peirce's epistemology, especially the way in which his view points the way out of scepticism.

This work is not intended to be a mere exposition. We have felt free to criticize and amplify Peirce's position. Most of our 'critical' remarks are favorable. Against Peirce, however, we suggest that abduction and induction are much more closely related forms of reasoning than he allows. We argue that induction collapses into a form of abduction – which, if true, is all the more to Peirce's credit, since it radically revises an age-old concept in a direction that he was the first to suggest.

Peirce is a delight to study. He argues in a "tough-minded" way for "tender-minded" conclusions. This kind of philosophical creature is a *rara avis*.

CHAPTER I

INFERENCE: THE ESSENCE OF ALL THOUGHT

Charles Sanders Peirce may be classed unambiguously among the "process philosophers," of whom there have been many in American thought – particularly James, Dewey, and Whitehead. A process philosophy has its peculiar advantages and problems, but Peirce applied the idea of process to the phenomenon of *cognition* in a truly radical and original way. For Peirce, the thinking of a thought, or the reading or hearing of a sentence, or even the perception of a sense datum, is analogous to hearing a musical phrase with the sense of flowing from note to note and the relief of the resolution at the end. In this first section we will examine this view – a view which characterizes thought as *inference* in contrast to *intuition* in the Cartesian sense.

The name of Descartes is of primary importance in this connection. Max H. Fisch has rightly said,

The castigation of Descartes – his faked universal doubt, his intuitions and introspections, his clear and distinct ideas, his dualism, his exaggeration of the ego, his mechanization of nature – has been a constant theme of American philosophy . . . Rightly or wrongly, all the evils of modern philosophy have been fathered upon him." [1]

Peirce was among the first of the American philosophers to attack the presuppositions of Cartesian thought. It was one of his very earliest philosophical themes. His famous paper on Cartesian philosophy, "Questions Concerning Certain Faculties Claimed for Man," appeared in the *Journal of Speculative Philosophy* in 1868, when Peirce was twenty-nine years old. This paper is worthy in every way of its author and betrays no youthful shallowness. Almost every study of Peirce's philosophy commences with an examination of this essay on "Faculties" and its sequels. This work will be no exception.

---

[1] *Classic American Philosophers* (N.Y.: Appleton-Century-Crofts, Inc., 1951), p. 20.

There are good and pressing reasons for thus commencing a study of Peirce. In the first place, Peirce's "Faculties" essays are among the very few of Peirce's writings in which he was able to stick very closely to his subject and to follow a line of argument straight through without long, if interesting, diversions, as was his usual habit. More important than that, the essays provide an exceptionally good introduction to many of Peirce's most basic epistemological positions. In them he questions, and very effectively questions, some of the axioms or cornerstones of Cartesian philosophy and, by extension, of most modern philosophy – at least up to his time.

Peirce's essays have as their main purpose the proof that all cognitions whatever are inferential in nature and not immediate and intuitional. All thought is in process; it requires time and is continuous. The implications which Peirce draws from these apparently small and trivial points are remarkable for their manifoldness and their suggestiveness. Peirce says that synthesis – the process of inference whence comes all new information – is the key to the door of philosophy. Whether that is true or not, it is certainly true that it is the key to Peirce's system.

It is interesting and important to observe that the doctrine that cognitions are or can be intuitive cuts clear across rationalist-empiricist lines. Traditionally, both of these schools have held to some form of intuition – either of first logical principles (the rationalists) or of raw sense data (the empiricists). Thus it is important to see how Peirce attacks the intuitionist theory and to have some understanding of what he is opposing, before one can hope to see his own alternative either clearly or sympathetically.

A. THERE WOULD BE NO TELLING OF AN INTUITION IF WE HAD ONE

In the first essay of this "Faculties" series, Peirce poses this question:

Whether by the simple contemplation of a cognition independently of any previous knowledge and without reasoning from signs, we are enabled rightly to judge whether that cognition has been determined by a previous cognition or whether it refers immediately to its object. (5.213)

This proposition is rather technically worded. Peirce's question is really this: Can we tell an intuition from other kinds of knowledge? A cognition that "refers immediately to its object" is an intuition, whereas a cognition that refers to previous cognitions represents a mediate kind of knowledge, as in all processes of deduction or inference. Peirce in his answer denies that we can distinguish mediate knowledge from alleged unmediated intuitions. He bases this denial upon the wider denial that we have any such thing as an unmediated intuition at all. When its implications are understood, this becomes a very shocking doctrine. Almost every philosopher has held that at least some of our knowledge must be intuitive. If all of our knowledge were mediated, there would seem to be an infinite regress; and knowledge would have no foundation from which developed and mediated knowledge could rise. Descartes held that we have intuitive knowledge of ourselves, and from this base all other knowledge could be developed. Kant, for example, held that the forms, e.g., of space and time, were forms of intuition – immediate and unmediated and fundamental to all other knowledge. And even the empiricists, who rail against other forms of alleged intuitive knowledge, themselves hold that the deliverances of our senses are the most immediate and fundamental sources of knowledge, and that these deliverances are unmediated by any other prior cognitions and therefore are intuitive. Murray G. Murphey rightly estimates the basic importance of this move of Peirce's when he writes:

> The denial of intuition is Peirce's boldest stroke against the British school, for Locke, Berkeley, and Hume all require the existence of intuition as an axiom. Thus Hume based his whole argument upon "our fundamental principle, *that all ideas are copy'd from impressions*," where by "impressions" is meant "all our sensations, passions, and emotions, as they make their first appearance in the soul." To deny this principle undercuts the whole *Treatise*.[2]

For Peirce, an 'intuition' is a "premiss not itself a conclusion." If one denies the existence of any intuitions, then every premise is itself a conclusion, drawn from other premises, and the chain of knowledge must go back indefinitely. Knowledge, in that case, would lack a sure anchor. Moreover, this means that synthetic or ampliative knowledge is not developed or grounded in the way mathematical or analytic knowledge is (wrongly) supposed to be. This, indeed, is the case for Peirce. In fact, for Peirce, this effort to ape the mathematical method has been the very root of philosophical mischief, and has led to most unfortunate consequences. One of these consequences is the effort to find axioms (intuitions) for all knowledge, axioms corresponding for all of our knowledge to Euclid's axioms in a small field of knowledge (geometry), and constituting an indubitable base and foundation for all other knowledge. The second major error, stemming from this effort to ape mathematics, is the attempt to

---

[2] Murray G. Murphey, *The Development of Peirce's Philosophy* (Cambridge, Mass.: Harvard University Press, 1961), p. 109.

make everyday knowledge as logically air-tight and certain as our knowledge of mathematical systems is (again wrongly) supposed to be. (Human or mechanical errors may be introduced into even deductive reasonings).

Peirce's position certainly requires defense, but it suggests right off a formidable objection to Descartes' view, even if the existence of his intuitions is granted: It suggests the question, can we intuitively distinguish between cognitions that are intuitions and others that are not? This Peirce denies. Historically there has certainly been no agreement on which of our cognitions are intuitive. Surely this is surprising if we really know them intuitively. Moreover, one can ask of any intuitive recognition of an alleged intuition whether it may be mistaken or not. To this question the only possible answer (within the framework of an intuitionist theory) is that it is intuitively certain that the intuition is correct. And this can itself be questioned *ad infinitum*. "Supposing that a man really could shut himself up in such a faith, he would be, of course, impervious to the truth, 'evidence-proof.' " (5.214) If there are no certain cognitive intuitions, it follows immediately that one cannot establish a bed rock upon which to erect human knowledge. The foundation itself may always be questioned. Thus, it is not a true foundation, for such could not be questioned. This argument, once properly understood and appreciated, can by itself make many of Peirce's most difficult doctrines become quite comprehensible and plausible. (This point concerning the infinite regress involved in the quest for certainty will be more fully treated in the section on "Signs" and later, in the section, "Knowledge grows organically," and finally and most thoroughly in our last section, "The Cartesian Circle.")

B. AS A MATTER OF FACT THE MIND WORKS INFERENTIALLY

Having shown that even if primitive intuitions occurred, we should have no way of identifying them, Peirce goes on to show that all *real* cognitions draw upon former ones for their significance, so that all premises are themselves conclusions. Peirce first points out the notorious difficulty witnesses have in distinguishing between what they have really seen and what they have inferred. Professional magicians depend for their living upon the mind's power or compusion to think in certain ways, ways determined by longstanding habit. Everyone admits that dreams arise from the association of ideas, which is to say from previous cognitions, and yet it is not at all uncommon for a person to become confused as to whether something really happened or was merely dreamed. So it is at least clear that even a dream, which as Peirce says, "as far as its own content goes, is exactly like an actual experience," (5.217) does not rely upon pure, primitive intuitions.

When Peirce speaks of an "inference," he means *any* cognitive activity whatever, not merely conscious abstract thought. Specifically, he includes perceptual knowledge and even subconscious mental activity. For example, everyone had once thought that the third dimension was immediately intuited, but now it is readily admitted that it is *inferred* from muscular adjustments in the eyes. The blind spot in the human eye, where the optic nerve enters the retina, ordinarily goes quite undetected and is filled up by the mind's power of "inference." (Anyone can make the experiment of placing a coin on a table a little to the left of his face, closing his right eye, and moving the coin back and forth while staring with the left eye at a spot directly in front of his face until the coin vanishes from his peripheral vision. The interesting thing to observe is that when the coin is removed and one continues to stare at the spot directly in front of one, there is no "black hole" observed in the blind spot, but the surface is completely filled in by the mind. No matter what color the top of the desk is, the bind spot will automatically take on that color. So adept is the mind at filling in this gap that, as this experiment shows, a special effort has to be made before we are even aware that it exists.)

The recent discoveries of Dr. Edwin H. Land [3] concerning the fact that the eye can "see" all the colors of the rainbow when, in fact, only two different wavelengths are present (and these may even be two different shades of the same color) *suggest* that somehow (no one now knows how) the mind is inferring all the colors from a very minimal amount of information indeed, and that the mind's power of "filling in" missing data is in this case almost incredible.

Again, "A man can distinguish different textures of cloth by feeling: but not immediately, for he requires to move his fingers over the cloth, which shows that he is obliged to compare the sensations of one instant with those of another." (5.221) This is an excellent point. Another particularly illuminating example is taken from our perception of tone. This sensation arises from the mind's noting the rapidity of the vibrations of the sound waves. The mind cannot tell a tone until it has had a chance to hear several of the sound impulses and judge their frequency. Thus the sensation of pitch is determined by previous cognitions. *One* oscillation of the air would not produce a tone! Peirce even argues successfully that our concept of two-dimensional space is not immediate,

[3] "Experiment in Color Vision," Edwin H. Land, *Scientific American* CC (May, 1959), 84-99.

but inferred. This is so because it is inconceivable that any single nerve ending on the retina could give the notion of two dimensional space, and therefore the concept comes from an inference from many single, discrete nerve endings.

There being, however, a very great number of nerve-points affected by a very great number of successive excitations, the relations of the resulting impressions will be almost inconceivably complicated. Now, it is a known law of mind, that when phenomena of an extreme complexity are presented, which yet would be reduced to *order* or mediate simplicity by the application of a certain conception, that conception sooner or later arises in application to those phenomena. In the case under consideration, the conception of extension would reduce the phenomena to unity, and, therefore, its genesis is fully accounted for. (5.223)

Thus Peirce has developed his argument both against the mind's having any immediate intuitions and against its having the capacity to identify them if it had them. The paper is so far very well argued.

C. KNOWING IS A PROCESS IN TIME

The fact, known to modern physiology, that tones and pains are cognized by the *frequency* of nerve impulses instead of by their intensity is particularly enlightening, because it brings to the fore the crucial role played by time in the cognitive process (as appears from all the above illustrations). According to Peirce's theory, all knowing is inferring, and inferring requires comparison throughout a span of time. Knowing is a *process,* which cannot be immediate and intuitive. Even something as apparently immediate and intuitive as pain is known only by a process of comparison, since the mind judges pain, like tone, by the *frequency,* not intensity, of nerve impulses. (But time is required to judge the intensity of pure quantity too).

In 5.284 Peirce makes the important point that *no* experience whatever is an "instantaneous affair, but is an event occupying time [4] and coming to pass by a continuous process." Instants are mathematical fictions. Moreover, *past thoughts* do not cease to exist instantaneously, but rather fade away ("gradually die out") and follow the law of association as long as they survive. The point which Peirce is raising here goes to the depths of his metaphysical theories, particularly synechism (continuity), to which we shall return. In part, these considerations on the knowing process support

[4] Compare on this point William James' essay, "Does Consciousness Exist?" – W.H.D.

a process metaphysics, and in part the latter supports the former, but it is crucial at this point to see at least that Peirce believes he has very good reasons for holding that all cognitions are inferences which require time – particularly so if time is in the warp and woof of the universe so that there is by the very nature of the case *nothing* which is not an *event*.[5] In Peirce's own words, ". . . from our second principle, that there is no intuition or cognition not determined by previous cognitions, it follows that the striking in of a new experience is never an instantaneous affair, but is an *event* occupying time, and coming to pass by a continuous process." (5.284)

D. THERE IS NO INTUITIVE SELF-CONSCIOUSNESS

Next Peirce raises the question whether we have an intuitive self-consciousness. Here, of course, he is hitting at Descartes' *cogito* doctrine, and this is perhaps a more difficult target. *On the surface* it seems highly probable that any sensation at all has as its logically necessary concomitant the idea of a mind or a self to be registering that sensation. Peirce would agree that the notion of mind is logically necessary, but not the notion of self. But in the case of pain, it is not merely some abstract mind that feels, but the pain seems to be in a quite irreducible sense *mine*. Of course it is not necessary to suppose that one is always consciously meditating on the fact that one is a self, but the mere analysis of the idea of a sensation seems logically to presuppose a feeling center peculiar to a mind. Unfortunately, a little examination shows that this problem is far more complex than Descartes' statement of it would suggest. First, Peirce hedges himself

---

[5] Cf. A. N. Whitehead, *Science and the Modern World* (N.Y.: The Macmillan Co., 1925), p. 159: "Physical endurance is the process of continuously inheriting a certain identity of character transmitted through-out a historic route of events." For Whitehead the forms of "eternal objects" are not events, but the physical and cognitive world are in process.

The question may arise as to whether Peirce is advocating a literally infinite continuum when he speaks of the cognitive process. Whitehead, who is most emphatically an atomist, holds only to a *potential* continuum in the cognitive process, or in any process. Peirce, however, is advocating a literal infinity of cognitions in any moment. (See 6.110f.: "It has already been suggested by psychologists that consciousness necessarily embraces an interval of time. But if a finite time be meant, the opinion is not tenable." Etc. See 6.134.) The issues raised here constitute a deeply puzzling metaphysical problem which we shall have to pass over. Neither the atomist position nor the "synechist" position is without baffling difficulties. The atomist usually supposes that around each electron, say, there is an electrical and gravitational field, the effects of which would be felt by all neighboring particles. But this field would presumably be spread out continuously and be felt infinitesimally at great distances. The "synechist," on the other hand, has to explain how his doctrine can be reconciled with quantum phenomena, which apparently deny infinitesimal forces.

For the purposes of this study we will proceed with an uncritical acceptance of Peirce's synechism.

about with a protective definition. He insists that this intuitive self-consciousness which people claim, be really a consciousness of *oneself*, "not a mere feeling of subjective conditions of consciousness, but of our personal selves." (5.225) This view of the matter might very well be far more strict than what Descartes either meant or needed – that is, Descartes may have only desired with his argument to show that the "subjective conditions of consciousness" exist. But by insisting on the strict view Peirce has little difficulty in showing that in babies, for example, a really developed sense of personal identity is quite late in coming. Peirce uses his famous argument that self-consciousness grows from an increasing awareness of ourselves as centers of ignorance and error. If everything always went our way (to put his argument a little differently than he does), if our merest wish served to accomplish the most amazing feats, we might never come to distinguish ourselves from the world (or even from God!). As it is, our failures and errors teach us about our separate existence. This argument, persuasive as it is, is not so effective, it seems to me, as an even simpler argument, as follows. Memory is necessary to a real *self*-consciousness (else it might be a new "I" that pops into existence every instant); but memory is fallible, and hence there is no *certain* intuition of *self*-consciousness. To all of this, Descartes could still reply: (1) There are thoughts, sensations, etc., (2) The notion of 'sensation' itself seems necessarily to imply some kind of mind or feeling center or analogous system (though that mind might not be the same one from moment to moment). *This* much might be indubitably certain. But whether this foundation is broad enough to support any further philosophical framework seems doubtful. In any case Peirce would deny that (2) above *certainly* follows from (1), for in any process of reasoning, no matter how simple or how purely deductive, a chance for error arises, and an error may have occurred between the thought of (1) and the apparently logically necessary concomitant (2). There are just *no* certainties for Peirce ("certain" being taken in its "metaphysical" or "ultimate" sense rather than its psychological sense). There may be the certainty of immediate feeling, but a feeling is no proposition, no knowledge. Only the immediate feeling is certain (and this, of course, is poetic language, since feelings are never spoken of as certain or uncertain; all that one can mean by this is that a feeling as felt *is felt*), but the proposition *that* there is an immediate feeling is not certain, for a thought (or, for that matter, a feeling) takes time (*Cf.* 5.284), and memory may fail during the lapse of time, or logical errors may creep in. Thus Peirce seeks to establish his doctrine that we have no intuitive self-consciousness, but that even self-consciousness is a complex inference.

We may observe here that Peirce also asks whether we have the power of introspection or whether our whole knowledge of the internal world is derived from the observation of external facts. People tend to think of introspection as an intuitive power. But Peirce points out in the first place that introspection need not be intuitive. (5.245) For the purposes of this essay, this is all he needs to affirm, and that he can affirm it in justice seems evident from some of the arguments he has raised already – for example, the very basic point that judgment takes time, and the mind uses the time in order to compare data, and any final judgment is therefore of the nature of an inference rather than an intuition. But Peirce, not satisfied with this, takes the bold step of denying that we have any power of introspection, properly speaking, at all. He points out that the emotions, which one might think we know by introspection, are really known by reference to external facts. For example, we say that *something* is vile or abominable, and, Peirce says, we attach the emotion to the thing, and not to our viscera. But this seems to ignore feelings such as ennui, or melancholy, where many times one cannot find any external cause for the feeling, nor think of anything to do to dissipate it. Peirce here seems to be arguing for too much. This discussion has given the commentators trouble. Gallie [6] passes it by in his discussion of this essay, and Buchler tries to elucidate Peirce's point in the hope of making it appear more plausible. Although his elucidation is accurate, it does not make the doctrine more credible. ("[Peirce] does not deny that we can carry on such examination [of the quality of feelings], but holds that in so doing we represent the feeling as the quality of an object, not as something purely psychical." [7]) The whole issue is unfortunate, since Peirce's main point can stand even with the power of introspection, provided only that it is not considered immediate and intuitive. (Is introspection more than the turning of one's attention to one's memory? It could be regarded as a form of remembering – remembering one's own feelings. Consciousness never succeeds in turning upon itself any more than a dog can catch its own tail. All consciousness can do is examine the immediate past. The examination of memories is certainly no more intuitive than the examination of anything else and no more infallible.)

[6] W. B. Gallie, *Peirce and Pragmatism* (Baltimore: Penguin Books, 1952), p. 66.
[7] Justus Buchler, *Charles Peirce's Empiricism* (London: Kegan Paul, Trench, Trubner and Co., Ltd., 1939), p. 15.

In an extended footnote Peirce argues that his theory against intuitions is not so far removed from Kant's epistemological views as might at first appear. Kant's theory of categories, being, as Peirce likes to call it, nominalistic (or subjectivistic), is therefore at root wholly unacceptable to Peirce, and yet a key word in Kant is "synthesis," where the mind harmonizes the deliverances of the senses into its forms. Kant certainly did not think of synthesis as a form of inference; but it is easy to see how Kant's synthesis can be conceived in a way not too far removed from Peirce's view of inference. Peirce says, in fact, that his theory is nothing but the detailed account of Kant's synthesis. (5.223n2) This is perhaps a little misleading, since for Peirce space and time themselves are synthesized (*Cf.* 5.223) and Kant's notion of synthesis is not as clearly formulated as Peirce's, which latter is found in his doctrines of induction and abduction. Peirce says:

There can be no doubt of the importance of this problem. According to Kant, the central question of Philosophy is "How are synthetical judgments *a priori* possible?" But antecedently to this comes the question how synthetical judgments in general, and still more generally, how synthetical reasoning is possible at all. When the answer to the general problem has been obtained, the particular one will be comparatively simple. *This is the lock upon the door of philosophy.* (5.348, my emphasis)

The very word 'synthesis' itself has the implication of a process of construction. For Kant, of course, there would be a difficulty in saying that a cognition is an event in time, since time, on his view, is itself a form of intuition and we cannot know about the mind as it is in itself. On the other hand, it is still true that on the "empirical" or "psychological" side (as Kant quaintly puts it) mental phenomena are in process and in time, for Kant. So it is true that there is some basic similarity here, although Peirce's statement that his theory is nothing but a detailed account of Kant's idea of synthesis is, as said above, somewhat misleading.

F. THOUGHT IS SIGN ACTIVITY

Some of the notions implicitly contained in the above remarks are made explicit in Peirce's sequel article called, "Some Consequences of Four Incapacities." In this article, Peirce gives his earliest formulation of his sign theory. The main point of the article is that all mental action, all inference, is a form of sign activity, where the word "sign" is interpreted very freely to include any "feeling, image, conception, or other representation."

(5.283) Most thinking, however, is conducted in signs that are "mainly of the same general structure as words." (6.338) (This is debateable, of course.) Now since all thought whatever is a process, it follows that mental action consists of a continuous flow of signs. (5.284) If the thought process were to be frozen and examined, nothing except an immediate feeling would be discovered (the "firstness" of thought); no "meaning" could be found. The reason for this is that a sign is not only a sign *of* something, but also a sign *to* some interpretant. (5.289) If there is nothing to interpret the sign, it loses its character as a sign. Therefore it is essential that *more* signs follow any given sign in order to interpret it.

At no one instant in my state of mind is there cognition or representation, but in the relation of my states of mind at different instants there is. In short, the Immediate ... runs in a continuous stream through our lives; it is the sum total of consciousness, whose mediation, which is the continuity of it, is brought about by a real effective force behind consciousness. (5.289)

A tune consists only in separate notes sounded one at a time. Alone, the notes have no significance; together, they may have a great deal. "Thought is a thread of melody running through the succession of our sensations." (5.395) The meaning of any sign is therefore entirely *virtual*, depending upon on interpretation. (5.289 and *cf.* 5.504n) In plain English, meaning always depends on context.

Peirce everywhere emphasizes the triadic nature of real sign activity. (*Cf.* 2.274) Reasoning, being sign activity, is also triadic in nature, and Peirce points to Aristotle and Kant as having vaguely seen this. (6.321 and *cf.* 1.372*f*.) There may be a real sign without an *actual* interpretant, so long as there is a *possible* one. (2.92) Obviously, a word in a book is a real sign while the book is not being read – but it would not be a sign without some possible mind in which it would arouse a cognition.

Interpretation must take place in a mind. (2.242) Peirce, however, does hint at the possibility of a non-mental interpretant, as when he suggests the possibility of a vegetable serving as an interpretant, and where he says that "*thought* is the chief, *if not the only*, mode of representation." (2.274, my emph.)

Peirce suggests there are three kinds of interpretants of signs. First is an emotional interpretation, as when the sign of music gives rise to a feeling. (5.475) Second is the energetic interpretant as in the response to a command. (*ibid.*) Third, is the "logical interpretant" which is a sign's repercussion on the ensuing thought life of the individual, and "ultimately" upon his habits of behavior. (In 4.536 he refers to these three types of interpretation as the "immediate," the "dynamic," and the "final" interpretants.)

The history of philosophy from Aristotle has recognized the "universal" character of ideas, as contrasted to the specificity of actual existences. In Peircean terms, every real triad (as a sign) involves "generality." Every genuine triad must "imply something concerning *every possible* object of some description . . . ." (1.476) Every idea to that extent is general, but all ideas have a further tendency to generalize: ". . . wherever ideas come together they tend to weld into general ideas; and wherever they are generally connected, general ideas govern the connection . . . ." (6.143)

For Peirce, thoughts are continuous. They do not break in suddenly, but gradually. They can start in time, but only continuously. (5.327) (Recall that one does not immediately hear a tone – the mind has to judge (not consciously, to be sure) the frequency of the vibrations. Here the cognition is starting in time, but continuously. A sine wave cannot start full-grown.)

Ideas are conveyed only by other ideas, and therefore if matter gives rise to ideas in our mind, that is a further proof of the ideality of matter itself. If, indeed, matter is "dead" and embodying eternal, unchanging laws (as it is not, for Peirce), even so, it conveys ideas to us only by virtue of the "spirit" it embodies. (6.158) On this point Peirce elsewhere speaks of the laws of nature as themselves being of the nature of signs. The immediate continuity of mental processes means that the past is never really past to a mind, but still really alive and present, only infinitesimally dying out. (6.134) No thought terminates suddenly. Our attention may shift suddenly, but the old thought fades away into the subconscious. Peirce says that an amoeba feels and that when it is irritated there is an active motion set up which slowly spreads through the organism, dying out while it spreads. (6.133) And, moreover,

Since space is continuous, it follows that there must be an immediate community of feeling between parts of mind infinitesimally near together. Without this, I believe it would have been impossible for minds external to one another ever to become coordinated, and equally impossible for any coordination to be established in the action of the nerve-matter of one brain. (6.134)

And again,

A finite interval of time generally contains an innumerable series of feelings; and when these become welded together in association, the result is a general idea. For we have just seen how by continuous spreading an idea becomes generalized.
The first character of a general idea so resulting is that it is living feeling.

A continuum of this feeling, infinitesimal in duration, but still embracing innumerable parts, and also, though infinitesimal, entirely unlimited, is immediately present. And in its absence of boundedness a vague possibility of more than is present is directly felt. (6.137f)

A man's self, his personality, consists in the unity of his mental processes: "Now the organism is only an instrument of thought.[8] But the identity of a man consists in the *consistency* of what he does and thinks, and consistency is the intellectual character of a thing; that is, is it expressing something." (5.315) [9]

Man's "glassy essence" consists in this process of continuous interpretation of signs. Thus, the sign is the man. (5.314) All thinking is a form of talking to oneself: the self of the present addresses the self of the future. (5.421)

There is no need to suppose that there must necessarily be some kind of deep mystery in saying that thought involves sign activity. A computer uses the "on-off" condition of thousands of cells in order to manipulate information, and puts this information out on sheets of paper full of signs. This is not strictly a mental phenomenon; but if there is a radical difference between living minds and machines, it probably does not lie in the fact that one uses signs and the other does not. Certainly the mind makes use of information stored somehow in the cells of the brain – and the alterations in these cells serve as signs. This is all true regardless of one's view of the mind-body problem.

On the other hand, one cannot say that the *particular signs* employed in the thought process *are* the thoughts. "Oh, no; no whit more than the skins of an onion are the onion. (About as much so, however.)" (4.6) Thomas A. Goudge suggests another analogy: ". . . the matter of thought is signs in the sense in which the chessmen constitute the matter of a game of chess." [10] Signs, says Peirce, are the phenomenal manifestation of ourselves: "This does not prevent [their] being a phenomenon of something without us, just as a rainbow is at once a manifestation both of the sun and of the rain." (5.283)

Peirce sometimes talks like a behaviorist, as when he says, "the man and the external sign are identical," or "my language is the sum total of myself;

---

[8] Contrast this with Bergson, Dewey, for whom thought is an instrument for the organism. W.H.D.

[9] Compare on this point Whitehead: ". . . the life of man is an historic route of actual occasions which in a marked degree . . . inherit from each other." *Process and Reality* (N.Y.: Harper and Bros., 1929), p. 137.

[10] Thomas A. Goudge, *The Thought of C.S. Peirce* (Toronto: The University of Toronto Press: 1950), p. 237. Actually, the clearest comparison is to say that thoughts are to signs what melodies are to notes.

for the man is the thought." (5.314) Goudge does not know what to make of this.[11] But when one understands Peirce's realism one understands that just as a chair *is* the *laws* of its behavior, so a man (or better, a man's character) *is* the habits, tendencies and dispositions which he embodies. Thus a man, taken as a self, a personality, a "spiritual" being, is the unity of his sign activity – not man taken as a body, a material thing. That this is a valid distinction to make is evident from Peirce's plain confession that he does not know how words influence the physical body. He says it is madness to deny that words produce physical effects. "But how thoughts act on things it is impossible for us in the present state of our knowledge, so much as to make any very promising guess; although . . . the problem is not beyond all hope of ultimate solution." (5.106) He then goes on to say that it is not any more clear how the laws of physics influence matter. He finally says:

> Here we have that great problem of the *principle of individuation* which the scholastic doctors after a century of the closest possible analysis were obliged to confess was quite incomprehensible to them. Analogy suggests that the laws of nature are ideas or resolutions in the mind of some vast consciousness, who, whether supreme or subordinate, is a Deity relatively to us. I do not approve of mixing up Religion and Philosophy; but as a purely philosophical hypothesis that has the advantage of being supported by analogy. Yet I cannot clearly see that beyond that support to the imagination it is of any particular scientific service . . . (5.107) [12]

In any case, it seems clear that Peirce recognizes the mind-body problem (though, of course, ultimately he is an idealist – still, body, as an effete kind of mind, is very different), and therefore cannot be called a behaviorist.

There is another very interesting problem in connection with Peirce's theory of signs. George Gentry raises it in an essay called, "Habit and the Logical Interpretant," [13] and Buchler also discussed it.[14] Gentry points to a much later essay of Peirce's, "A Survey of Pragmaticism," (1906) where Peirce says that the logical interpretant of a sign is "essentially" a *habit*. Peirce says in this essay that "it is no explanation of the nature of the logical interpretant (which, we already know, is a concept) to say that it is a concept." A concept is a logical interpretant, but "only imperfectly so."

---

[11] *Ibid.*, p. 238.

[12] But neither is the notion of matter of any scientific service; it is only a "support to the imagination" too! W.H.D.

[13] In *Studies in the Philosophy of Charles Sanders Peirce,* Philip P. Wiener and Frederic H. Young, edd. (Cambridge, Mass.: Harvard University Press, 1952), pp. 65 *ff.*

[14] Buchler, *op. cit.*, pp. 112 and 154.

A concept, as an interpretant, "partakes of the nature of a verbal definition, and is as inferior to the habit, and much in the same way, as a verbal
definition is inferior to the real definition." But a *habit* "is the living definition, the veritable and final logical interpretant." (5.386 and 490)

To Gentry this later position is a radical revision of the earlier view that
the interpretant of any sign must be another sign. Gentry considers the
later theory that the final interpretant of a sign is a habit as much the
better one in that it frees one from the infinite "regressus" and "pro-
gressus" involved in the notion of the continuity of signs.[15]

It appears to us, however, that it is easy to show that Peirce had no
notion of revising his early theory by this later exposition. His consistent
position was that a concept is known by the habit it produces, but the most
important habit which a concept produces is not an external habit – a
habit for "doing" – but rather a habit for thinking. To be sure, concepts
have practical, outward implications, *a la* James' theory. But they also
have implications for the further thought-life of the individual – some
being fruitful (i.e., with a high unifying power) and some not. How signs
influence the body and have their "practical" effects, he has already confessed he does not know. But these physical effects are unimportant compared to the effect which a concept may have on the mind's further search
for the truth. To put the matter plainly, ideas and habits of thought are
more important than deeds. This is a commonplace. And as for the problem of an infinite regress and progress, Peirce holds that thoughts not only
spread within an individual's mind, but also between the minds of different people. He holds that the whole universe, for that matter, is
continuous, through and through, so if one cannot accept Peirce's doctrine
of synechism (continuity) one cannot follow him very far. The problem of
an infinite regress of signs is a sub-problem under the problem of continuity
in general. Synechism is a metaphysical doctrine with wide implications
reaching far beyond our topic. It suffices in this context to say that Peirce
defended it by trying to show the fallacy in Zeno's paradoxes. There was
for Peirce no more mystery attached to the problem of how a thought
begins than there was to how a movement of any kind begins – and no less.
(*Cf.* 5.333*f.*; 6.177*ff.*)

It is really not such a difficult thing to believe that all knowledge is, or
may be, in a continuum of some kind. Readers familiar with Whitehead's
so-called fallacy of "misplaced concreteness," will recall that he objected
to the doctrine that *things* must be at some *one* place and could not be
everywhere at once. Things, rather, are everywhere they act, and they act

---

[15] Gentry, *op. cit.,* p. 89.

everywhere. If reality is *in* a continuum, as Peirce, Whitehead, and modern physics seem to suggest, why can't mental reality be in one too? In fact, if physical reality is in a continuum, how can mental reality *avoid* being in one? That ideas are continuous is much easier to imagine than that matter is continuous, and the latter is pretty well established.

It follows from Peirce's doctrine that no thought can be considered as intuitively clear, simple and perfectly self-explanatory. All thoughts require other thoughts to make them clear, and these thoughts require others too. Now if there is no such thing as an intuition – a firm foundation for all deductive or ratiocinative knowledge, a basis, clear, indubitable, and axiomatic, then we are either lead into a complete scepticism, or to an alternative something like Peirce's.

Thus we must consider the possibility that knowledge may be essentially circular, or if not circulair exactly, then involving some kind of infinite regress, and lacking an axiomatic basis. At one point, talking about the relation between "evolutionary love" and the continuity of thought, Peirce drops this remark: ". . . the two propositions will lend one another mutual aid. The reader will, I trust, be too well grounded in logic to mistake such mutual support for a vicious circle in reasoning." (6.314)

This remark contains the basic idea: all ideas and signs are understood only in terms of other ideas and signs, and these in terms of others, till at last one meets the original ones again. The case is precisely analogous to an effort to discover what is the "key" organ in the human body, what is the cornerstone of life. Clearly the heart is nourished by the lungs and stomach, while they in turn are fed by the heart and blood. The brain lives off of the vital fluids supplied to it by all of these organs in concert, while it serves to bring the body in the proximity of external sources of food, and take the body from sources of external danger. In short, the body is an organism. In a similar fashion the inferences of the mind do not rest on primitive axioms, but mutually support one another. The most famous case of this mutual support is perhaps found in the fact long-observed that induction depends upon the orderliness of nature, which, itself, is known by an induction (or, rather, abduction, I would say – see below).

The image might be changed from that of an organism to one that brings out other features characteristic of the knowing process. Perhaps the knowing process involves something on the order of a jig-saw puzzle, where each new bit adds significance to the whole, although each bit is incomplete in itself and there is no real foundation piece upon which all else is based. *Any* piece will do to start with, where nothing is infallible in principle, though much does not fail in practice.

Philosophy ought to imitate the successful sciences in its methods, so far as to proceed only from tangible premises which can be subjected to careful scrutiny, and to trust rather to the multitude and variety of its arguments than to the conclusiveness of any one. Its reasoning should not form a chain which is no stronger than its weakest link, but a cable whose fibers may be ever so slender, provided they are sufficiently numerous and intimately connected. (5.265.3)

Whatever the exact truth is in these matters, Peirce has shown almost conclusively that it is nothing like what Descartes had in mind. Even if knowledge is not absolutely continuous, it may be virtually so. Gallie asks whether it is possible to determine precisely when a person begins to speak, walk, or have his first thought. There is no way of answering such a question in fact and maybe not even in principle. Is a word uttered *accidentally* "speech," or in simple, uncomprehending *imitation,* or with only the vaguest intimation of what it stands for? Where does imitation leave off and "speech" begin? One probably cannot draw such a line; for a baby the intimations of meaning simply grow stronger and stronger.

In summary, this essay raises some most primitive questions, and the answers suggested to them intimate the whole of Peirce's philosophical viewpoint. It is important to observe that the attack on Descartes is meant to undercut virtually all of philosophy since Descartes, insofar as subsequent philosophy has tended to work from these same essential Cartesian presuppositions in one form or another. All of these later philosophers looked for some sure foundation of knowledge, whether relying upon "rational insight," or clear and distinct ideas, or the alleged immediate deliverances of sense. All of these philosophers share an exaggerated respect for deduction, and a disregard for the facts of common sense, with the exception, naturally, of the common sense philosophers.

Anyone who understands and sympathizes with Peirce so far is in a good position to follow him further as he works out some of these ideas. Peirce's system is highly interdependent, and the commentator faces the same difficulty Peirce himself did – the difficulty of explaining or discussing any one theory or thread of thought without showing how the whole system bears on the problem and, in most cases, makes Peirce's suggestions much more probable than might seem to be the case at first glance. Almost every essay Peirce wrote wound up being a summary of his whole system, with emphasis on one of its facets.

CHAPTER II

HYPOTHESIS OR ABDUCTION:
THE ORIGINATIVE PHASE OF REASONING

We have already seen that Peirce, in his early "Faculties" essays, refers to cognitive processes of *all* types as "inferences." (*Cf.* 5.237) The point of these essays is to deny that there is any such thing as an immediate intuition of any kind, and the word "inference," or, better yet, "synthesis," represents well his alternative view that all cognitive processes are *movements* of the mind from one thing to another. He compares thought to music in that its essence involves movement and that it has a natural end, i.e., belief and habit (both habits of action *and* habits of *thought*). For Peirce, there are three kinds of reasoning processes: deduction, induction, and abduction. Some of his greatest insights are found in his understanding of these modes of thought, and much of his philosophy is implicit in his explication of them. There are, however, certain very important clarifications and perhaps even improvements which can be made over the way Peirce sees the matter.

A. DEDUCTION, INDUCTION, AND ABDUCTION

Deduction and induction Peirce understands roughly in the traditional way. Abduction, however, is the creative act of making up explanatory hypotheses. It is a mental process of the greatest possible importance, because it is more basic than the two traditional forms of reasoning. This so-called "abductive" process was the object of the most careful study on Peirce's part, and a very fruitful inquiry it was.

There are some interesting things to say on the subject of Peirce's view of deduction, but for the moment it suffices to remark that it is generally orthodox. He agrees with tradition that deduction is analytic in essence and that no really new information is to be got by using it. Synthetic knowledge, new information, can come only from induction and abduction. Now, although Peirce goes to great lengths to show the difference between these latter two forms of synthetic reasoning, it is not the case even for Peirce that they are entirely different and separate from each other. They are very much akin to each other, and there is a strong tendency, as we will try to demonstrate, for induction to collapse into a form of abduction, so that one can almost say that all synthetic forms of cognition, including perception, induction and invention, are abductive.

But first, let us play the devil's advocate and emphasize the differences one might claim between induction and abduction. Peirce plainly declares that the two are not to be confounded (2.632), and also comments upon the ease with which one can "distort" hypothetic inference (abduction) "into the appearance of induction." (2.642) (Observe that this is the opposite of the reduction which we are tempted to make.) Peirce goes to the trouble of listing four reasons for maintaining the distinction between these two forms of reasoning. (2.641-2.644). The first is that induction is a much stronger form of inference than abduction, since a creative hypothesis can be wildly wrong, whereas, it is harder for an induction to be completely and totally wrong. Second is the fact that induction reasons from certain observed facts to postulated facts *of the same kind* ("I have drawn such and such a proportion of red beans from the bag; probably the same proportion holds troughout."), while abduction points to a fact of a different kind altogether, a fact which presumably unifies many diverse facts. Napoleon's real existence is an abduction which explains many facts. Induction, traditionally understood, hardly makes this kind of leap, but contents itself, says Peirce, with judging a proportion. (*Cf.* 2. 642) Thirdly, there is an important "physiological" difference between the two, inasmuch as induction yields a *rule* or a *habit* while abduction yields a mental unity with an accompanying sense of relief, and is thus the "sensuous" (2.643) element of thought rather than the "habitual." And finally, if we distinguish between induction and abduction, the classification of the sciences is facilitated, according to Peirce. That is, "classificatory" sciences are inductive, and "theoretical" sciences (geology, biology, etc.) are hypothetic. (*Cf.* 2.644)

Despite Peirce's reasons for distinguishing between induction and abduction, I believe it can be shown that one must finally recognize that these two forms of reasoning are really similar in an even more fundamental way. Peirce himself virtually admits this in several passages. He says,

... when we stretch an induction quite beyond the limits of our observation, the inference partakes of the nature of hypothesis. It would be absurd to say that we have no inductive warrant for a generalization extending a little beyond the limits of experience, and there is no line to be drawn beyond which we cannot push our inference; only it becomes weaker the further it is pushed. Yet, if an induction be pushed very far, we cannot give it much credence unless we find that such an extension explains some fact which we can and do observe. Here, then, we have a kind of mixture of induction and hypothesis supporting one another; and of this kind are most of the theories of physics. (2.640)

It appears to us, however, that instead of speaking of a "mixture" of induction and abduction, one ought rather to say that every induction *involves* an abduction, though an abduction of a low order of creativity. Thus induction is more properly viewed as a *form* of abduction. If so, our understanding of induction is greatly modified and the problem of establishing its validity as a form of reasoning can be attacked more intelligently.

In accordance with the above suggestion we may say, when beans are drawn from a bag and the relative frequency of their colors is noted (to take a favorite example of Peirce's), it is an abductive leap, an hypothesis, to say that the same proportion probably prevails throughout the bag. Induction proper is then merely the determining of the proportion found in the sample and at most the notion can be expanded to include the testing of the hypothesis that the same proportion probably prevails throughout by drawing out more beans and seeing if the proportion is preserved. Peirce says in 5.171 that "Abduction is the process of forming an explanatory hypothesis. It is the only logical operation which introduces any new idea; for induction does nothing but determine a value, and deduction merely evolves the necessary consequences of pure hypothesis." But if abduction is "*the only* operation which introduces any new idea," (and we agree that it is) then it seems one ought to say that it is the *only* truly *synthetic* operation. This is what we have always meant by synthetic reasoning. Induction, on this view, becomes really only a form of what Peirce calls "probable deduction" – as when one deduces from the premise, "Three-fourths of all men are colored; here is a man; therefore, the chances are three out of four that he is colored." An induction is an hypothesis which occurs to one who has examined statistics. Inductions, as we say, are not greatly "creative" hypotheses, but they are or involve hypotheses for all that. Another place where Peirce almost inadvertently lends support to our view that abduction is the only creative act of mind is in 2.624 where he says:

Induction is where we generalize from a number of cases of which something is true, and infer that the same thing is true of a whole class. . . . Hypothesis is where we find some very curious circumstance, which would be explained by the supposition that it was a case of a certain general rule, and thereupon adopt that supposition.

The fact that the word "general" is common to both of these sentences is what is suggestive, for a kind of generalization occurs in both cases. One certainly does not "generalize" in the usual sense of that term in deduction (or, if this is contested, we may gladly admit the other side too, since that would support the kinship of deduction with abduction, which is an idea susceptible to profitable development). Peirce ordinarily used the word "generalization" to refer to induction narrowly conceived, as when one generalizes from a sample to all phenomena *of the same kind*. One does not "*generalize*," he says, to Napoleon's existence. (*Cf. 2.714*) One *hypothesizes* that. But generalization in this narrow sense (which for the sake of the argument we can grant is the common usage of the word, though one might argue it) is still just a form of hypothesis-building. As Peirce himself argues, induction *always* serves to *test* an hypothesis. "Induction is an Argument which sets out from an hypothesis, resulting from a previous Abduction, and from virtual predictions, drawn by deduction, of the results of possible experiments, and having performed the experiments, conclude that the hypothesis is true in the measure in which those predictions are verified...." (2.96, my emph., *Cf.* 5.145, 170, 590-591; 2.755, 77, 6.472, 527, 100, and 7.202*ff.*) And again Peirce says: "The one primary and fundamental law of mental action consists in a tendency to generalization.[1] Feeling tends to spread; connections between feelings awaken feelings; neighboring feelings become assimilated; ideas are apt to reproduce themselves. These are so many formulations of the one law of the growth of mind." (6.21)

In summary, *new* knowledge comes through abduction – induction and deduction serve to test abductions. We are happy to be in agreement on this point with Buchler, who, though he passes over the point lightly, nevertheless very clearly says: induction and abduction "are not independent, and the conclusion of any induction is identical with that of some abduction, that is, it is some hypothesis. *Any* synthetic proposition, in so far as it is for the first time entertained as possibly true, must be the result of an abduction." [2]

---

[1] Notice that Peirce uses the word "generalization" here in a way contrary to what he suggested was the proper usage above. W.H.D.

[2] Justus Buchler, *Charles Peirce's Empiricism* (London: Kegan Paul Trench, Trubner and Co., Ltd., 1939), p. 134, and cf. Goudge, *op. cit.*, pp. 197ff., where he suggests much the same conclusion on this matter.

These considerations are of a more fundamental nature than the reasons Peirce advanced for distinguishing between induction and abduction, and it is a very attractive abduction, indeed, with much explanatory and unifying power, to suppose that induction is really an elementary and almost mechanical form of abduction, and that synthetic reasoning and abduction are the very same process.

But if this view of the matter is true, it is not something to be commented upon and left to the side. It has, on the contrary, astounding implications for epistemology. It draws our attention away from Euclid, Descartes, Mill and the whole modern school of logicians and their hangers-on. It draws our attention away from excessive efforts toward analysis, where the effort is made to get out of our minds what is already there implicitly, which we already know to be little enough and confused enough. It turns our attention to the need for new *insights*. It makes us look again at Whewell, the speculative philosophers, the artists and creators of all kinds, and the giants of science. It turns out attention to the problem of creativity, so long neglected (because so difficult) and so long ridiculed (because feared). Just as the sciences have not outgrown their need for imaginative and creative minds, minds capable of inventing new and powerful hypotheses, so philosophy needs minds capable of inventing new explanatory and unifying concepts. Analysis is only a preliminary to this main need and not an end in itself.

There is, to be sure, a steadily growing awareness that science is not, and philosophy should not be, an inductive or deductive process, but rather an *abductive* one – a matter not of mechanical calculation but of creative insight. But the awareness has certainly not been encouraged by the still prevelant tendency to view deductive logic as the model of all important reasoning, when the opposite is the case. "It is regrettable," says Paul Weiss, "that the logicians are not yet ready to follow Peirce into this most promising field" (of abduction).[3] The implications of the importance of creative insight in the life of the mind have indeed not been developed as they ought, but perhaps it is the very fact that mechanically oriented minds have all too well sensed the implications of this approach that they have shied away from it. The fear certainly exists that once the artist has been let in the door the priest will not be far behind.

Speaking of the greatest men of science Arthur Koestler writes: "The themes that reverberate through their intimate writings are: the belittling of logic and deductive reasoning (except for verification after the act);

---

[3] "Charles S. Peirce, Philosopher," in *Perspectives on Peirce,* Richard J. Bernstein, ed. (New Haven: Yale University Press, 1965), p. 125.

horror of the one track mind; distrust of too much consistency . . .; scepticism regarding all-too-conscious thinking." [4] Koestler quotes Max Planck as saying that "the pioneer scientist must have a vivid intuitive imagination for new ideas not generated by deduction, but by *artistically* creative imagination." [5] English philosophy with its hypnotic and paralyzing facination with the methods of deductive logic only dreams that it partakes of the scientific spirit. Indeed, folksingers have a better claim to that.

It is no use saying that Peirce was a logician. "Logic teaches us," he said, "to expect some residue of dreaminess in the world, and even self-contradictions." (4.79)

B. A SUGGESTED SOLUTION TO THE PROBLEM OF INDUCTION

We have already argued that abductive thinking is involved in the inductive process, and hence that induction is not the mere gathering of statistics and mathematically determined probabilities, but is rather a truly inventive and creative form of reasoning. We wish here to elaborate at length on this theme and to see what illumination this insight may shed upon the classic problem of induction. We are convinced that this way of viewing the matter has very significant implications for this grave and difficult problem.

Whatever contribution the following remarks may make to our understanding of this problem rests of course upon the suggestions made by Peirce and discussed in the preceeding section. But although Peirce suggested these remarkable new insights, he was unfortunately far from seeing the significance of his own suggestions and actually committed the worst possible mistake – namely, that of supposing that inductive inference, by itself and independently of any prior knowledge or hypothesis concerning the nature of the whole, could lead us to a probable knowledge of the nature of the whole. Hume proved that this could not be done, and no one has or can prove otherwise. But we will discuss this point in its place.

Peirce's contribution to this subject, as indicated, consists in his powerful suggestion that all synthetic knowledge comes from abductive reasoning, that is, the coming of a creative insight into the problematic situation, the appearance of a plausible hypothesis. And induction, in so far as it gives us new information, does so by virtue of the fact that *behind each induction is an hypothesis,* a governing insight, not proved, not arbitrarily

[4] Arthur Koestler, *The Act of Creation* (N.Y.: Dell Pub. Co., 1964), p. 146.
[5] *Ibid.*, p. 147.

postulated (as Reichenbach would have it [6]), but rather felt or divined. This is the key to understanding the inductive process, and to answering Hume's objections to that process insofar as those objections can be answered.

Now let us state the problem of induction in its starkest form. Let us imagine that we have been ushered into a room and this room is full of stacks of playing cards, full up to the ceiling, with only small access passages through the stacks. Now imagine that we start drawing cards off of one of these stacks, one at a time. Suppose that we continue doing this for hundreds of cards, until we are, say, halfway down one of these stacks. And suppose further that each card that we turn up is an ace of spades. Now, we pause to ask, what do we *know* about what the next card may be? The next card is a brand new event. It has no necessary connection with the cards that have gone before it; it has no probable connection with them either. The next card, for all we know, may be a trey of clubs, a king of hearts, or, for all we know again, it may have the Lord's Prayer printed on it, or it may have a shiny surface in which we see our own faces, or it may be entirely blank. In short, it may be any of a literally infinite number of things.

Now it is true that we will probably tend to *feel* that this next card will be an ace of spades, since all of the preceeding cards have been. But now we must ask exactly *why* we will feel this way. According to Hume, if there is anything in the whole universe which we know, which we know surely and positively, it is this: that, for all we know, there *may be* anything whatever on this next card; and, in addition to that, among all this infinity of things which might be on this card, we have not the least idea which among them will be more likely to be on the card. The cards that have gone before have no connection direct or indirect, upon the nature of this new card. For all of the bearing which the previous cards have on this next card it may be literally anything in the world which can be got on that size card.

But if we know, if we positively and certainly know, that anything whatever may be on that card, why do we feel that it will probably be another ace of spades? The answer to this, according to Hume, is simply that we have developed a habit of expecting to see aces of spades turn up. It is a sheer matter of habit, of animal expectation, of custom. But of course the habit which has been built up in us will not have any effect

---

[6] Cf. Hans Reichenbach, *The Rise of Scientific Philosophy* (Berkeley: The University of California Press, 1966), pp. 244-246. Reichenbach of course does not use the word "arbitrary" but that is what his view amounts to since any good reasons we might have for our inductive posits would themselves depend upon induction, in his view.

upon the nature of that next card any more than the previous cards will alter its nature. It is a new event, and neither what has gone before nor our expectations will change its nature or even have any bearing on its nature.

Moreover, according to Hume, all of our knowledge of the so-called "laws of nature" stands upon the same logical footing as our knowledge of these stacked cards. For example, we have seen (or heard reports of) the sun come up countless thousands of times. So, assuming the accuracy of history and our memory, we know what has characterized the past. But what do we know about the chances of the sun rising tomorrow? Nothing. Tomorrow is a new day. What bearing on tomorrow has the fact that the sun came up one morning one thousand years ago? Or came up a whole week in a row a thousand years ago? Or came up yesterday? Or came up today? Or has come up for as long as men know about? None, says Hume. Tomorrow is a brand new event, wholly independent of the past events.

Hume believed that this position was unassailable, that it was positively airtight, and I am in the position of agreeing with Hume, except for saying that these same facts can be interpreted in a manner which throws something of a new light on the situation.

But we must be clear about what Hume is saying. He is saying that all of our alleged knowledge of the "laws of nature" is, strictly speaking, perfectly useless for purposes of prediction. We do not know, not even probably, that fire will continue to burn or heavy objects fall or any such thing at all. Our ignorance of the future is *complete and entire*. Hume admits, of course, that we don't feel that way. We *feel* that the floor will support us if we take a step, that oxygen will continue to nourish us rather than poison us if we breathe. But this is a mere feeling, a habit or custom, and as such is entirely unsupported by any *reasons* whatever. As a feeling it is very powerful indeed, but it is wholly irrational. Thus we are led to a complete scepticism.

Properly the so-called "problem of induction" concerns the kind of *a posteriori*, existential induction which this example involves. *A priori* induction, the kind of induction delt with by mathematicians is, on the contrary not problematic at all, but is a science as strict and rigorous as the deductive sciences of geometry or algebra. The mathematician will talk, for example, of a deck of cards. If one draws a card from a deck of ordinary playing cards at random, the chances are one in four that one will draw a club. From the mathematician's point of view this is quite accurate, but we see at once that the mathematician is making several presuppositions which, in all strictness, he must be called upon to justify. He is assuming such things as the following: that the deck is an *ordinary* deck (and if he has not examined it beforehand, he doesn't know but what it may be a trick deck of some kind, and if he has examined it, he doesn't know but what somehow the cards are able to change their spots), that our perception of the cards will be "normal," i.e., that we are not under some kind of hypnotic spell which causes us to see all playing cards as hearts, etc., etc. But we see from Hume's analysis, that what happens even with these playing cards depends upon the continuance of all the usual laws of nature, but these themselves are known only by induction, which means that they are not known at all but only felt. If the general laws of nature are not known but only felt, then all of the specific events within the general framework of nature, the tossing of dice or the drawing of cards, can not be reasoned about inductively unless the general framework can be supported.

On the other hand, it is true that if we presuppose the validity of the general laws of nature, and thus that our perception of the cards will be normal and the cards themselves will behave normally, then the mathematician's calculations are sure and certain. (Though these calculations are, of course, only of a probability.)

But the reason that the mathematician's calculations are sure and certain lies in the fact that he already knows some very important characteristics of the group from which he is drawing samples. He already knows how ordinary playing cards are marked and he knows that the deck is normal and the drawing is random. If you walk him into a room piled full of playing cards, as in our first example, he will not be able to make any better prediction about that enigmatic next card than anyone else, simply *because he does not know the characteristics of the collection as a whole.* The next card may have a mirror on it or the Lord's Prayer. He has no idea and can have no idea unless he gets some information or hint as to the characteristics of the collection as a whole.

All of this can be made somewhat more clear with the example of a bag of beans. In drawing beans out of a bag, all depends on what, if anything, we know about the whole. First, do we know it is a bag full of *beans?* If not, the drawing out of a bean, proves nothing about what may come out next. Second, do we have any reason to believe that the beans have been evenly distributed? If not, the drawing out of 5,000 red beans proves nothing about the next beans to come out because the bag might have white beans in its bottom half and red beans in its top half, or any of an infinite number of other combinations. But if we know that the bag is full of beans and that they have been evenly distributed, then our notion of the characteristics of the beans still in the bag is improved with the drawing of each new bean, and all the laws of inductive reasoning apply. But until we know some important characteristics of the whole, inductive reasoning, from the standpoint of the strict mathematics of the case, *can not work,* can not tell us anything at all about the future.

We can, however, make up hypotheses, guesses, and use them in the place of any specific knowledge. If we know nothing specific about the whole – that is, have not the least hint about its characteristics as a whole and thus find ourselves quite unable to make even an "educated" guess, we can make some sort of guess using as our basis the most fundamental feeling we possess about the nature of the universe in all its parts: the notion of order and simplicity. If we start drawing from a bag and we have no fore-knowledge whatever about the contents of the bag, and we (1) draw a red bean, and (2) are somehow *forced* to make some guess as to the rest of the contents of the bag, then, using our criterion of order and simplicity, but without any other reason whatever, we may hazard the guess that the next thing we will draw out of the bag will be a red bean. If it turns out to be a white bean, we may then guess that there are 50% red beans and 50% white beans in the bag. If the next object to come out is a weevil, we may revise our guess, using the same criterion, to 33% red beans, 33% white beans, 33% weevils, etc. Of course we may find a banjo in the bottom of the bag. Nothing is proved. Nothing is even probable unless our hypothesis of order was correct. If there was some order induction will tend to reveal it, as mathematics can prove. If there was no order (i.e., each thing taken out of the bag is different, and there is no principle governing the selection or order of these different things), induction is powerless, and will never yield a correct prediction.

Thus those are wrong who say that the mere fact of continuing to take samples long enough will uncover for us the nature of the whole. That is not true unless (1) we know something about the whole to begin with, or (2) the whole is finite and we will eventually take all the samples – but in this case we are not reasoning at all but merely observing, not making a prediction about future experience.

Up to this point in our discussion, the things we have said have served merely to reiterate Hume's view, particularly by making clear the fact that induction can work only when some important characteristics of the whole are known, or supposed. Usually it suffices if we know that the whole is uniform or regular and our samples are random or representative. (Incidentally, it is often claimed that induction will work even without the supposition that the samples are representative. The idea being that the samples *must* become representative after enough of them are taken. This is Donald Williams' point, on which more below. But to see that this is false, imagine a bag full of a fifty-fifty mixture of wheat and small iron pellets. Now begin to withdraw samples from this bag with a magnet! The sample *must* be representative: this is the whole basis of induction.)

It has long since been observed that induction will work if we can know that the universe is uniform and our samples of it representative. But the only way we have of knowing that it is uniform is by judging from our past experience of it, in short by an induction. Thus the validity of induction for general scientific purposes depends upon – the validity of induction! Thus, we have no sure foundation for our postulate of uniformity and order. If we had somehow got some experience with several universes, then we might be able to characterize them in general – i.e., gain some knowledge of the whole, upon which to base our inductions, as a mathematician knows the characteristics of a deck of cards. But since we have had no experience whatever with universes, and moreover do not know the characteristics of our own universe as a whole, we have no *reason* (in the deductive sense) for presupposing or taking as a postulate the notions of order, uniformity, and simplicity. Once again, we only know a certain sample of our universe – but without a prior knowledge of the whole, such a sample gives no indication of the nature of that whole. On the other hand, as Hume pointed out, our protoplasm, our cells, force us to *feel* this way – to expect regularity, because our protoplasm obeys the laws of association, takes habits, and the ordered features of the sample of the universe which has so far impressed itself upon us, has given rise to this set of animal expectations. We have no *choice* here as to how we do feel. It is not a matter of reasoning and reasons in the deductive sense of those terms.

It will be objected that this whole analysis commits the gravest circularity at this point where it affirms that protoplasm takes habits, i.e., that we suppose that nature is uniform for the very poor reason (or good reason) that we can do no other – we are made to think that way. The circularity will be said to enter in here because we may ask, "How do we know that protoplasm takes habits, except from an inductive inference? And what if protoplasm were to suddenly cease to have this characteristic?" This is a helpful question, and it will be illuminating to consider it.

The answer is as follows: indeed it is true that we know no more about the future behavior of protoplasm than we do about the future of the laws of nature in general. We may have a completely different set of animal expectations in the future, starting in the next second for all we know.

That is to say, we *may* very suddenly cease to be habit-taking creatures, and thus suddenly cease to believe in the regularity of nature.

But in the meantime, if we can agree that so far at least we have had such habits and expectations, we must also admit that one of the things which our habits lead us to expect is that *they themselves* will probably not change suddenly any more than the course of the universe as a whole will be subject to sudden alterations or changes in its fundamental laws.

Thus, what our habits make us expect of other things they also make us expect of our habits themselves. And the one is no more irrational than the other. We see at once that much is going to depend upon what one means by irrational (or rational). If one means by rational, "able to be *deduced* wholly or probably, from things already known," then our expectations are irrational. But if we believe that in the last analysis all of our reasonings reduce to a simple yielding to feelings, then our expectations of uniformity and regularity are rational. Of course we take the latter view since, as it seems, if we do not call rational one of the most fundamental beliefs which we have – the belief in the uniformity of nature – then we can call nothing rational. But we do call various things rational and irrational, and if all of our rationality reduces itself to a species of irrationality, still there remains quite a big difference between things that are "irrational" in a way that thoroughly satisfies our basic feelings, and things that are irrational in a way that does not; i.e., there is a difference between things that are rational and irrational, to lapse back into common parlance.[7]

We see already from this analysis of induction and the meaning of "reason" what considerable truth there is in those who approach the problem of induction from the standpoint of linguistic analysis. It all *does* depend upon what we mean by "justification," "good reasons," etc. But this approach is lacking in that it goes no deeper than in merely determining how we use such words and what we really mean by them. But there are *reasons* why we use such words the way we do, even if these reasons are ultimately based upon feelings. If we call induction "reasonable," it is not that we have arbitrarily attached this word to this way of thinking. One doesn't solve the problem of induction and justify it as a way of thought by merely declaring that we simply choose to call such

---

[7] Consider the following remarks by A. C. Ewing: "Yet we cannot suppose it irrational to believe that if we jump from a height we shall fall; and even if we say that all induction is in some sense irrational, it will still be incumbent on us to explain the distinction between scientific inductions and those inductions which would be accepted by no sensible person. What is the difference between the two kinds if they are both irrational?" A.C. Ewing, *The Fundamental Questions of Philosophy* (London: Routledge and Kegan Paul Ltd, 1951), p. 168.

thinking reasonable and justified. There are *features* of this kind of think-ing that distinguish it from other (sloppy) kinds of thinking – thus we sometimes call an induction reasonable and the expression of a prejudice unreasonable. The reason for this distinction has to do (in part at least) with the degree of subjective satisfaction involved, taking into account the degrees of satisfaction involved in the past practical effects (i.e., whether it works or not) as well as the satisfaction involved in being able to get others to agree with us. These latter are (by comparison) more external criteria than our simple feeling on the matter considered alone and by it-self, though this is fundamentally important too.

All of this so far is pure Hume. However, toward the beginning of this discussion we promised something of a new interpretation of the facts which Hume has called to our attention. The point to be made is essential-ly this: contrary to Hume and contrary to practically every epistemologist since him *scientific reasoning does not depend upon induction at all!* Nor does it depend upon anything so simple as our ability to take habits. The rising of the sun as an example of inductive reasoning is drastically mis-leading by its simplicity. Scientific reasoning, indeed all of our reasoning, depends upon the mind's ability to have insights, to see things coherently and harmoniously, to see laws and principles, in short, to make up hy-potheses. Hume has misled generations of philosophers because he utterly ignored the place of hypothesis in human thinking. Perhaps it is enough that he should have seen the vast importance of the law of association. But when someone grasps the principle behind the workings of some machine or of some feature of nature, he is *not merely being impressed by a succession of regularities,* he is not merely gaining a habit. He is having an insight, seeing principles, grasping interconnections. This is the feature of our mental life which was so wonderfully emphasized by Peirce, but Whewell, long before, saw the same truth.

The following example shows that the crux of scientific thinking or thinking in general is not inductive (much less deductive), but abductive, i.e., consists in having an insight. In fact, we may go so far as to say that hardly any scientific discovery of any importance rests upon simple in-duction, but rather is a matter of seeing laws and principles. The follow-ing illustration is crucial to our exposition of this point.

Imagine a black box which presents one with little slips of paper one at a time as each one is withdrawn. We withdraw the first slip of paper and find on it the number "one." If we are going to use simple, statistical in-duction to predict the mark or marks on the next piece of paper, if indeed it is to have a mark, we must say that so far as we know the chances are one out of one that the next slip of paper will have "one" marked upon it. This involves the hypothesis that in the markings there will be some order or principle or regularity, for if we do not presuppose that, then we have not the remotest idea what will appear on the next slip of paper, if anything will appear there at all. But we have long since seen that all inductive reasoning, if it is to have any validity at all, must presuppose order and regularity. (In fact, it must not merely presuppose it, but know it, if it is to have any deductive validity, and in the present case we do not know that there will even be any more markings on the papers at all, much less what they might be if there are any.) But now let us examine the next slip. On it we find the following notation: "two." Now by inductive reasoning (as it is commonly misunderstood) we must suppose that the chances are fifty-fifty that the next card will say, "one" and the chances are fifty-fifty that it will say, "two." But in fact we find that the next card says, "three." Obviously, if the cards are going to name off all of the positive integers one after another our simple, statistical inductive inference will *always be wrong.* But only a fool would say, after seeing the numbers one through ten come up, that the chances are one in ten that the next slip will read "one," one in ten that it will read "two," etc. By this time we will have had a probable insight into the situation. It will certainly not be an infallible insight, and indeed *it will be quite strictly impossible to attach to it a probability figure,* and yet we sense the appropriateness of predicting that the next number will be "eleven." Of course the machine might start recycling and go back to "one" again. Or it might come up with "three." It might be the Lord's Prayer. It might be anything we can imagine. But we *sense* that some predictions are more appropriate than others.[8] But a numerical value *can not be attached to an "appropriateness."* [9] And

[8] The most appropriate guesses would probably be the following, in order of likelihood; "eleven," "one" (on the hypothesis that the machine will recycle), and "nine" (on the hypothesis that it will go backwards to "one" again). One could imagine other possible patterns, but from the given data they would all be very unlikely.

[9] It is interesting to note that Arthur Pap, after an exhaustive review of proposed solutions to the problem of induction, comes to a very similar conclusion. He says: "Our critical survey of attempts to measure the probability of universal hypotheses and of actually practiced methods of justifying acceptance or rejection of a statistical hypothesis without ever using the expression "probability *of* the tested hypothesis" points to the conclusion that, whatever may be meant by the "high probability" or "high degree of confirmation" of a universally quantified proposition, it cannot be a magnitude amenable to calculation by the laws of probability. If so it will be impossible to justify a certrain [sic] method of inductive generalization by showing that a hypothesis h that is made in order to account for data e and in order to guide further predictions has a high numerical probability relative to e. It does not follow, however, that we are never justified in saying that h is *well confirmed* by e in a nonquantitative sense ..." p. 236f. (*An Introduction to the Philosophy of Science,* N.Y.: The Free Press of Glencoe, 1962). Pap does suggest that we can be justified "in a nonquantita-

therefore this type of reasoning is not at all related to mathematical induction. In fact, the reasoning involved is not reasoning at all in any deductive or mathematical sense, but is an insight, which ultimately is a reliance upon feeling, to which all reasoning in the final analysis reduces, even deductive reasoning.

At this point we may consider an objection. It may be said that induction will work in this case because the sample reveals that each new event has the character n plus one, and thus if the box is going to put out all the positive integers in succession, instead of our prediction always being wrong, as I asserted, it will, on the contrary, always be right. And this is certainly true. The point, however, to be observed is simply that the grasping of this "n plus one" hypothesis is something done by the mind. The physical sample itself is absolutely neutral as to what kind of hypothesis is appropriate. *The sample waits upon an interpretation.* In some situations (e.g., drawing beans from a bag) we would take the simplest hypothesis as the most attractive one – i.e., in the present case, the hypothesis that the chances are one in ten that any of the first ten integers will come up next. In some contexts, perhaps even this one, we might guess that the machine is going to recycle – thus our guess for the next card would be "one," not "eleven." Mathematically speaking, deductively speaking, we simply have no idea in the world as to the next event. This is what Hume proved. This is true because the possibilities are infinite. But we realize that if there is going to be any kind of order at all in the presentation of the cards, that some kinds of order will be more simple and thus, subjectively speaking, more attractive and likely-seeming to us.

In other words, the data is there -- ready to be *interpreted.* And interpretation is creative, uncertain, dependent upon our feelings and sensitivities, and in the last analysis not subject to conclusive proof (though sometimes subject to virtual disproof). It is not true of course that one interpretation is as good as another. Some are stupid, awkward, inappropriate, and unreasonable. From the data which our imaginary machine has put out one might come to a theory predicting the following series of integers: 1, 3, 5, 7, 9, 1, 4, 8, 1, 5, 1 – and then recycle. This is a rather too sophisticated hypothesis to call it stupid, but it is still pretty unlikely and strained. The criterion of awkwardness and unreasonableness is unavoidably subjective.

---

tive sense" in calling some inductions well confirmed. I have tried to explain just how this is so. Pap urges upon us, however, a purely linguistic solution to the problem. I have already mentioned my reason for viewing this type of solution as arbitrary and unenlightening.

In short, *every induction involves some sort of interpretation of the sample*, some sort of hypothesis about the whole, and to such hypotheses and interpretations we can never attach a probability figure, but only a feeling of confidence. This is why induction in its broad sense of existential reasoning can never be treated successfully in a purely mechanical way. It is always an hypothesis which supplies the "knowledge" about the whole upon which all inductions depend. And this is no knowledge in the sense that it is either an experienced fact nor a deduced truth, but rather it is a *guess,* a stab, an hypothesis. It is a creative probe into the unknown. It is based upon nothing else but our feel for the situation, our sense of appropriateness. It is more like divination than mathematics. It is quite fallible. In fact there are no "reasons" whatever for placing any faith in our sense of appropriateness except for the following, if they be reasons: (1) this sense of fittingness is often overwhelming; (2) our minds may be co-natured with reality, in a general harmony with it, and thus a reasonably reliable guide to it (Peirce's point). The first is no "reason," but an appeal to animal propensities, and the second, if we were to try to defend it, would involve a circular argument – i.e., we would be arguing from a scientific hypothesis to support the validity of scientific reasoning in general.

Now let us consider the "reasons" which lie behind our interpretation of nature as uniform: In the first place, we may as well admit that there is an element of habit involved in this belief. But sheer habit does not always suffice for belief, particularly when we see some reason why the expected usual event will not occur. Our actual thinking about the regularity of the universe is somewhat more complex than a matter of mere habit. We may perhaps more or less subconsciously make the following considerations: (1) If there is a God who plans to bring the curtain down upon this physical universe as soon as it has served its purpose, it does not seem likely or reasonable (notice *seem*) that He would be interested in making minor repairs or adjustments in the present system of physical law. Any change likely will be very radical and amount to the end of the physical universe altogether. But if this is going to happen, we can have no idea of when it may happen, and so, outside of being religious, praying, etc., we may, for worldly purposes, plan as if it were not going to happen. (2) If there is no God, it is hard to see why or how the present system of physical laws could change, allowing, however, the possibility that new manifestations of the present laws might somehow develop and appear, e.g., some kind of superman with, say, fantastic powers of telepathy. So we may say that the uniformity of the present universe will probably be preserved as long as it (the universe) lasts. And from this basis of uniformity we reason scientifically. Thus, our belief in the uniformity of nature is not an induction any more than are most of our scientific hypotheses, but it is rather an abduction.

In any deductive sense, we should have to confess our utter and complete ignorance concerning such matters as these, just as Hume said. And yet we do hazard hypotheses which seem to some degree appropriate or reasonable to us. A little thought will reveal that all of the difficulties which seem to present themselves result from that old fallacy of taking deductive reasoning as the model of all our correct reasoning, when deduction is useless for the purpose we most need our minds for, i.e., to divine what is unknown. In deduction we merely elaborate on what is already known, and thus only clarify and unfold what we already knew implicitly, but gain no new information. And induction, understood in its usual, mathematical sense is nothing but a form of deduction (as follows: (1) Any sample taken from this whole will have approximately the same features as the whole. This is merely assumed, or it is known to be the case because precaution has been taken to assure the representative nature of the sample. (2) This sample has the feature x in the proportion y. (3) The whole will have the feature x in approximately the proportion y. This is deduction in form, no matter what it is called.)

Similarly, an hypothesis is formed in the case of inducing the nature of beans in a bag. If we have a bag and one red bean has been withdrawn from it, we make a guess, depending upon the total context of the situation – a guess as to whether there is anything else in the bag at all, or whether there may be other objects in it besides beans, or whether, if there are beans in it, they are all likely to be of the same kind or not. In the overwhelming number of cases where one might be in a situation of drawing beans from a bag, one would hypothesize that the bag is full of beans of exactly the same kind as those or the one drawn. If the circumstances were extraordinary, one might go ahead and make up an appropriate hypothesis, but one would probably have much less confidence in its validity.

Actually, all of these are simple facts, and not such as to strain anyone's brain. Only God, if there be a God, knows when the world will end, if it will end, or when there will be a radical change in the system of natural law, if there will be such a change. We can not attach probability figures to such alternatives, much less prove anything. We can only *know* inductive probabilities when we know some characteristics of the whole from which our sample is being taken. If we know the whole is uniform then we can draw some conclusions. But we have no experience with universes, nor do we know any of the characteristics of ours beyond the sample we have taken. So far as deduction or classical induction are concerned, to-morrow is all unknown. The sample proves nothing about the whole unless we have some reason to believe the whole is somehow like the sample. The sample itself provides no such information, and the sample is our only source of knowledge on the point, and thus there's an end to discussion on the point. This conclusion is inescapable.

It would be a very great task indeed to go through all of the efforts which have been made to justify inductive reasoning upon deductive principles of some sort. But they can all be refuted by keeping firmly in mind one great truth and applying it ruthlessly to each new suggestion. That truth is this: we do not know what the future will be like or even if there will be a future. We can only guess.

To show how this works we may examine a particular case of reasoning. Here in one longish sentence is a very clever and persuasive effort to ground induction upon *a priori* grounds:

By saying that we draw the inference *provisionally,* I mean that we do not hold that we have reached any assigned degree of approximation as yet, but only hold that if our experience be indefinitely extended, and if every fact of whatever nature, as fast as it presents itself, be duly applied, our approximation will become indefinitely close in the long run; that is to say, close to the experience *to come* (not merely close by the exhaustion of a finite collection) so that if experience in general is to fluctuate irregularly to and fro, in a manner to deprive the ratio sought of all definite value, we shall be able to find out approximately within what limits it fluctuates, and if, after having one definite value, it changes and assumes another, we shall be able to find that out, and in short, whatever may be the variations of this ratio in experience, experience indefinitely extended will enable us to detect them, so as to predict rightly, at last, what its ultimate value may be, if it have any ultimate value, or what the ultimate law of succession of values may be, if there be any such ultimate law, or that it ultimately fluctuates irregularly within certain limits, if it do so ultimately fluctuate.

It is with sad tears that we must confess that this passage was written by Charles Sanders Peirce. (6.40) From a literary standpoint the passage has much merit. Philosophically, it is brave. But the proposition it expresses is false. It is false because no matter what ratio past experience has established, this ratio tells us absolutely nothing about the experience to come. In the first place, it does not tell us, either absolutely or probably, whether there will be any experience to come at all, much less its character. This fact alone *conclusively* destroys this argument. And in the second

place, supposing that experience will go on indefinitely, no matter what ratio past experience established (and it will always establish *some* ratio, contrary to Peirce's implication – even if each event is totally different) this ratio gives us no logical (deductive or pseudo-deductive) warrant for believing that any future event will be like the past one or ones. The next event is all unknown. No matter what pattern past events have disclosed, no matter how long those events have persevered in that pattern, we cannot make a statement of probability concerning the next event with any degree of assurance from the standpoint of deduction or statistical induction unless we know some important characteristic of the whole, for the next event may mark the beginning of a totally new pattern, or even the beginning of chaos, and unless we know something about the whole from which we are drawing samples, those samples will not necessarily indicate anything whatever about the remaining portions of the whole, if there be any remaining portions. There is no possible counter-example to refute this view of the matter. For whatever example is given, a simple act of the imagination will suffice to name a new event which is not predicted by the ratio which the given sample has disclosed, and, unless we know something about the nature of the whole, whatever we imagine will be as likely to happen as anything else we imagine, including the event which the ratio predicts.

The reason Peirce wrote such a sentence as the one quoted was because he was importing the notion of abduction into his mind and thinking partly of it.[10] If experience presents us with a pattern, we will take that pattern as an hypothesis. If it presents us with no pattern, or no seen pattern, we will be at a loss to make a hypothesis, and thus at a loss to make a prediction. But there is nothing whatever in the *mathematics* of such a procedure – the procedure of making up a plausible hypothesis – which guarantees a tendency toward accuracy of prediction. In fact, mathematico-deductive reasoning is a very specialized form of reasoning in general and would not ordinarily suffice even to enable a man to make up an hypothesis. Understanding a principle (as that behind the piston engine) has very little in common with deductive reasoning. Nor does mathematics help us when we speculate as to the likelihood of nature remaining uniform. Nor does induction have anything to do with the making up of hypotheses. As we showed above, mere statistical induction could not even predict the next number in a series of integers. Induction, in all

---

[10] Cf. Goudge's extensive treatment of Peirce's position on probability and induction, and his conclusion: "The result is a muddle on the term 'probable,' as may be seen most obviously in regard to induction." *Op. cit.*, p. 177.

cases, depends upon a previously made hypothesis, or a previously *known* feature of the whole. One has to see a principle. The only way we can possibly justify placing any reliance upon the hypotheses we make concerning the future is by supposing the truth of another hypothesis: namely, that the mind is in harmony with nature and can divine nature's truths in a rough way. (A pragmatic justification will not do because what *has* worked may not work in the future, and it is the future which is in question.)

In another place Peirce wrote,

My own theory is that in inductive reasoning the fact stated in the conclusion does not follow from the facts stated in the premises with any definite probability, but that from the manner in which the facts stated in the premises have come to our knowledge it follows that in assigning to a certain ratio of frequency the value concluded we shall be following a rule of conduct which must operate to our advantage in the long run.[11]

There are two or three things to notice here. First, Peirce acknowledges that inductions do *not* give one "any definite probability." This is important. It is just our point that it is *abductions* which are said to be vaguely "likely," and this is also true of inductions insofar as they are really abductions. In the long quotation previously given Peirce hints again at this same point that inductions yield no mathematical ratio when he says, "By saying that we draw the inference *provisionally,* I mean that we do *not* hold that we have reached any assigned degree of approximation as yet ..."

But when is this "as yet"? After a few phrases Peirce begins to speak of "close" approximations, and "ratios," and "definite values" of ratios, etc. But after how much experience do these things emerge? Not "as yet," evidently. But when our experience is "indefinitely extended." And when is that?

The truth is of course that we can have nothing but a subjective assurance that we are achieving a "close approximation," or a "definite ratio," and that for the reasons already outlined. But Peirce gets credit for sometimes sensing that he needs to avoid the suggestion that induction will give a mathematical probability.[12]

[11] Item 766 in the microfilm copy of the Peirce MSS. No date.
[12] See Chung-Ying Cheng, "Charles Peirce's Arguments for the Non-probabilistic Validity of Induction." *Transactions of the Charles S. Peirce Society,* III, 1, Spring 1967, pp. 24-39. Cheng gives a good critique of Peirce's assertions that a world without discoverable uniformities is impossible, and that even in a world without law that would be its law. See also *Transactions,* III, 2, Fall 1967, Gordon N. Pinkham, "Some Comments on Cheng, Peirce, and Inductive Validity," pp. 96-107.

Moreover, in the quotation above Peirce speaks of "the manner in which the facts stated in the premises have come to our knowledge." Both Peirce and Donald Williams (see below) are most vague on the problem of how one insures that one's sample is fair without having *a priori* knowledge of the nature of the whole. To quote Cheng again,

A fair sample, according to [Peirce], is one which is chosen according to a method which would lead us to obtain sample of the population with equal frequency in the long run. But, I have argued that either no such method can be known with certainty, or the existence of such a method must be ascertained on the basis of induction.[13]

Let us briefly glance at one more example of an effort to ground induction upon mechanical, deductive, or mathematical principles. Donald C. Williams in 1947 published a book, *The Ground of Induction,* in which he attempted to show that induction will succeed independent of any hypotheses concerning the whole. This book constituted one of the greatest efforts of moderen times, perhaps of all time, to give an *a priori* grounding to the principle of induction. The book in many ways is a wonderful production, but it entirely fails of its object. The reasons for this failure were immediately pointed out upon the publication of the book by Dickinson S. Miller in an article in *The Journal of Philosophy* (Vol. XLIV, No. 25, Dec. 4, 1947, pp. 673-684).

We may go at once to the heart of the matter with the following quotation from Williams' book:

In the first place, although the inferring of the composition of the population from the composition of the sample is not logically the same as the converse process of inferring the composition of the sample from the composition of the population, both inferences could be made valid by the single general principle that given any population and any (largish) sample thereof, it is highly probable that the sample matches the population (and hence that the population matches the sample). In the second place, the latter general principle may be proved to be true by no more intricate method than considering *the whole range of possible population compositions* and observing that although the probability of a matching sample of a stipulated size is different for different compositions, the probability of a matching sample is always greater than the probability of any other kind of sample, and if the sample is large, then *no matter what the population composition may be,* the probability is very great. (p. 88)

In this quotation we find three unwarranted, and unproveable suppositions. First, that our known data is only a sample and not the whole itself.

[13] Chung-Ying Cheng, *Peirce's and Lewis's Theories of Induction* (The Hague: Martinus Nijhoff, 1969), p. 159.

That is, the present data gives no indication whatever that there will be more data forthcoming. Thus, we do not know that there will even *be* a tomorrow, much less the probability that the sun will take its accustomed course. We do not know that the card coming out of the black box will have anything on it, much less the probability of what will be on it. Second, we do not know that we have a "largish" sample, unless we know something important about the size of the whole. If our black box has put out a thousand cards with "one" written on them, what will appear on the next card is, from the standpoint of strict induction, *entirely* unknown. In this case we would indeed have an hypothesis, a guess. But it would be based on no deductive, *a priori* principle whatever. (And Williams claims his principle is *a priori*.) The next billion billion cards may have "two" written on them. They may have anything or nothing written on them. Even if our sample (a thousand cards) is largish – i.e., the machine only puts out a total of one thousand one cards, we have not the least *a priori* warrant for assigning a probability to any possible marking on the next card. If we imagine that it is somehow "probable" that the next card will have a certain mark on it, that can be only because we believe we have some insight into the nature of the machine and how it works, what principle it is constituted upon. Third, he assumes that we can consider the "whole range" of possible population compositions, and thus arrive at a probability figure. But in real experience this "whole range" is literally infinite, and where it is not infinite that can only be because we already have some knowledge concerning the whole. Thus, in our black box example, anything whatever might be written on the next card (and "anything" includes all the positive integers which are infinite in number). *It is precisely this ever-present infinity of possibilities which destroys our ability to establish a probability figure.* Miller expresses these criticisms of Williams' position in the following clear language:

Inasmuch as in the cases that arise in induction the possible other members of the class are for us wholly uncertain in existence and, if existent or so to be, wholly unknown in character beyond being members of the class, we have no assurance, not even any degree of probability, in the matter. I speak, of course, from the strictly deductive point of view, which alone is here in question.[14]

In this last sentence Miller is hinting that there *is* an appropriate way of reasoning about such matters, and indeed I believe there is. But it is creative, not mechanical. It is appropriate, fitting, satisfying, natural, not deductive nor (insofar as classical induction has been a form of deduction)

[14] *Loc. cit.*

inductive. One makes hypotheses, and hopes that one's feeling for the situation is not all wrong. Thus strict induction of the sampling kind could never predict the next figure on the cards coming from our black box in the simple case where the cards gave the positive integers in succession, but any child would quickly see the principle being used and predict accurately.

It is interesting that late in his career Bertrand Russell modified his views on the problem of induction in the direction of the conclusions of this study. His new position is fairly close to the position of this study:

My belief about induction underwent important modifications in the year 1944, chiefly owing to the discovery that induction used without common sense leads more often to false conclusions than to true ones.
. . . .

It has been usual to suppose that non-demonstrative inferences depend upon induction. This, however, is not true, except in a carefully limited sense. The inductions that scientists are inclined to accept are such as to commend themselves to what may be called common sense.
. . . .

... There are, in fact, an infinite number of formulae which will fit any finite set of facts ... Pure induction, if valid, would lead you to regard all these formulae as probable, although they contradict each other.
. . . .

... I conclude that induction, in so far as it can be validly employed, is not an indemonstrable premiss, but that other independent premises are necessary in order to give the necessary finite probabilities to inductions which we wish to test. The conclusion is that scientific inference demands certain extra-logical postulates of which induction is not one.[15]

Albert Einstein, no mean authority, writes in the same vein: "There is no inductive method which could lead to the fundamental concepts of physics . . . . in error are those theorists who believe that theory comes inductively from experience." [16]

We conclude therefore that inductive reasoning in its broadest application has not been and cannot be justified upon a deductive, mechanical model. Thinking and reasoning are essentially *creative* processes and go beyond all of our efforts to write logic books. Deduction and induction are tools which scientists use. Sometimes it is helpful to deduce some conse-

[15] Bertrand Russell, "non-Demonstrative Inference and Induction," in *The Structure of Scientific Thought,* Edward H. Madden, ed. (Boston: Houghton-Mifflin Co., 1960), p. 323.

[16] Albert Einstein, *The Method of Theoretical Physics* (Oxford, 1933), quoted in Norwood Russell Hanson, *Patterns of Discovery* (Cambridge: At the University Press, 1958), p. 119.

quence from a hypothesis for testing purposes. Sometimes it is helpful to take extensive samples. But the heart of scientific discovery is the same as discovery and invention in any field. It is a matter of creative insight into laws and principles.

C. ABDUCTION AND EXPLANATION

We have tried to demonstrate that induction, when it seems to give mathematically sure probabilities, is depending upon some insight, hypothesis, or guess as to the nature of the population in question. These antecedent hypotheses themselves cannot be judged as having such and such a probability. They can only be judged as appropriate, fitting, satisfying to our sensibilities or not. This is, no doubt, the despair of the logicians, but it is the final, inescapable fact for all that, and it is the way scientists and in fact all men actually think.

The problem of induction thus reduces to the problem of "abduction," or successful hypothesis-building. How is it possible for the human mind to come to a true hypothesis, when there are always an infinite number of wrong hypotheses from which it has to choose? We have already hinted at the direction in which we would look for an answer to this problem, but it opens up a theme beyond our present topic. Suffice it to say that behind every induction, whether we understand by this word the narrow phenomenon of gathering statistics or the broad phenomenon of scientific, existential reasoning in general – behind every induction is either a known characteristic of the whole or an hypothesis as to that or those characteristics. And the problem of induction becomes the problem of hypothesis.[17] Having shown the relation that exists between abduction and induction as this latter has been traditionally conceived, the way is now open to show in more detail what the process of abduction is supposed to be.

As has already been suggested, "abduction" could be regarded as a new word for a very old philosophical insight. And this insight is that the mind has a tendency to seek out the unifying features which phenomena exhibit. This apparent thirst of the mind for unity and coherence is most persistent. The quest for unity is of great intensity, and seems to lie at the very root of the system-building tendency in philosophy, as well as at the root of physical researches, or, really, of intellectual activity of any kind. The quest of the mind for comprehensiveness is not, as some have suggested, pernicious, but rather it is of the essence of the life of reason. Peirce at one

---

[17] See John J. Fitzgerald, "Peirce's Theory of Inquiry," *Transactions of the Charles S. Peirce Society*, IV, 3, Fall 1968, pp. 130-143 for a very good summary of Peirce's classification of various forms of inductive inference.

point says that "the function of conceptions is to reduce the manifold of senuous impressions to unity and . . . *the validity of a conception* consists in the impossibility of reducing the content of consciousness to unity without the introduction of it." (1.545, note well the phrase we have italicized.) And again he says, "It is a well known law of mind, that when phenomena of an extreme complexity are presented, which yet would be reduced to *order* or mediate simplicity by the application of a certain conception, that conception sooner or later arises in application to those phenomena." (5.223) The importance of this "law of mind" is evident. What we have here is not induction in the traditional sense of that word, for one does not *induce* the existence of Napoleon from various monuments, documents, etc. We are dealing with a creative leap of inference, far more constructive and far more liable to error than an induction from simple enumeration of things. The heart and soul of the matter is the *unity* the mind finds in a good hypothesis. The craving for a unified view of things is as real as any of man's physical cravings, and more powerful than many of them. Peirce says that "hypothesis produces the *sensuous* element of thought, and induction the *habitual* element." (2.643) Whenever the nervous system is disturbed in a complicated way, says Peirce,

. . . the result is a single harmonious disturbance which I call an emotion. Thus the various sounds made by the instruments of the orchestra strike upon the ear, and the result is a peculiar musical emotion, quite distinct from the sounds themselves. *This emotion is essentially the same thing as a hypothetic inference,* and every hypothetic inference involved the formation of such an emotion." (*Ibid.*, my emph.)

This is a very wonderful insight. Why a unified conception or a good hypothesis should give rise to a satisfying emotion, while poor hypotheses, on the contrary, tend to irritate, is a difficult problem indeed, which Peirce answers in terms of his theory of instinct.

It is necessary to see that for Peirce *all* sensations or perceptions partake of the nature of a unifying hypothesis. Peirce says, "A sensation is a simple prediate taken in place of a complex predicate; in other words, it fulfills the function of an hypothesis." (5.291) Sensations can be and usually are almost infinitely complex as they are presented "raw" to our brains. The sensations received by the player of table tennis are not only very complex, but the time in which he has to unify them in his mind and judge appropriate responses is very limited. Yet in an almost miraculous way the mind harmonizes the data and makes appropriate reactions with fantastic ease. Although the same principle applies to every act of perception, it is especially easy to see the abductive process at work in the phenomenon of ordinary vision where the mind does so much filling in and inferring in a creative way. Everyone of us has had the experience of seeing a drawing or a photograph which, at first, made no sense at all. The mind struggles to get a grasp on the scene, and finally, as if in a flash, the connection and harmony becomes apparent, and we see what the drawing or photograph is of. During the period of confusion, all of the data were present; all that was lacking was an hypothesis, an interpretation of the data. This is a striking example of abduction on the level of ordinary perception. Peirce uses the example of music to good effect on this point too. We never *hear* a melody. We only *hear* a tone or set of tones at a time. To hear a melody memory and anticipation must work together with the presently heard tones. Thus in even so simple an act as listening to a melody the mind is called on to fill in creatively. In the case of extremely foreign or strange music it is unable to do this, and the mind cannot determine what the melody is even though it hears all the notes! (*Cf.* 5.395*f.*)

If it seems strange when Peirce says that even ordinary perception is an inference from premises to a unifying conclusion, Peirce has an explanation for this: ". . . a fully accepted, simple, and interesting inference tends to obliterate all recognition of the uninteresting and complex premisses from which it was derived." (7.37)

Now, bearing in mind the point made in the preceding section, that abduction and induction are similar and that there is some justification for arguing that induction is a form of abduction, notice that Peirce says of induction itself that it is a "species of 'reduction of the manifold to unity.' " (5.275) And then, after discussing abduction, Peirce concludes that "it is . . . also a reduction of manifold to unity." (5.276)

These quotations serve two useful purposes: First, they support our point that induction and abduction are very fundamentally related forms of inference because they both reduce a manifold to unity. Second, they show that the heart of the matter, the heart of the hypothesis-building process, and thus of all synthetic knowledge, is found in this effort of the mind to reduce complexity to harmony and unity. That the mind can so often succeed in its effort to do this proves something about nature to a realist like Peirce – namely, that nature is a harmonious whole and has achieved already a degree of "reasonableness." But more importantly, Peirce's notion of abduction bears closely on the question of what constitutes a good hypothesis. Certainly *one* characteristic of a good hypothesis is that it brings harmony to a complex situation, or "reduces a manifold to unity," to use the Kantian phrase. In fact Peirce says, as we pointed out above, that the very *validity* of an idea consists in the fact that without it certain data could not be reduced to a unity. (1.545) There is, of course, much else to be said on the subject of what constitutes a good hypothesis, but this one thing is surely fundamental and important.

Before abandoning this rather general discussion of abduction, there are two or three other points which may help us understand more clearly what Peirce means by abduction. First, abductions typically "come to us in a flash." (5.181) An abduction "is an act of *insight*, although of extremely fallible insight." (*ibid.*) All of the component ideas in an abduction may have been present in the mind before the abduction was made, but the *new combination* of ideas, or the *relation between them* is what is new in an abduction. Perhaps the most common example of abduction, where its nature stands out, is in the experience most people have had at one time of solving problems in geometry, and trying to devise proofs. Sometimes one had to stare at the problem for some long period of time before the *whole solution* appeared before the mind's eye in a moment of "insight."

Secondly, although abduction is thought of as a creative leap of the mind, this does not by any means imply that the leap has never been made before by anyone or that it is original in the history of human thought – although indeed new theoretical discoveries are abductions. But abduction also properly describes the situation in which one man is trying to explain something to another, and the latter finally – perhaps after repeated hearings of the explanation – exclaims, "I see!" Thus, when a man "catches on" he has performed an abduction. An abduction, or a "catching on," is accompanied by a sensuous quality already mentioned – the sensation of harmony and unity which the mind has upon seeing things a certain way so that they fit together naturally.

It seems clear that Peirce's line of thought is well worth pursuing in that, first, the matters under discussion are of basic philosophical importance, and, secondly, Peirce's suggestions as developed so far at least, are provocative. But at this point they raise as many questions as they solve.

For example, what about this "sensuous" element to the abductive process, whence does it arise, and what does it prove, if anything?

Perhaps the most fundamental point to consider in discussing abduction is that for Peirce the whole essence of *explanation* is contained in the phenomenon of abduction. Every explanation is an abduction and vice versa. In one place (1.487) Peirce says, ". . . it is to be assumed that the universe has an explanation, the function of which, like that of every

---

[18] John F. Boler, *Charles Peirce and Scholastic Realism,* (Seattle: University of Washington Press, 1963), p. 87.

logical explanation, is to unify its observed variety." In 2.636 he says that induction classifies, and abduction *explains*. Boler [18] says:

Peirce is even tempted to say that only abduction explains, although he modifies this to some extent. He feels that an explanation requires something other than the facts to be explained (6.273), and since neither deduction nor induction supplies a new idea, each fails to do anything more than restate the facts themselves.

The modification to which Boler refers is that sometimes "Peirce seems to allow for a looser sense of explanation that includes induction." [19] This is not surprising in view of the vague line Peirce sometimes draws (unnecessarily!) between induction and abduction.

The great *plausibility* of Peirce's understanding of the nature of "explanation" seems to hide the greatness of his theory. The theory is so good that it appears obvious and almost not worth saying. But it is an art that conceals art. To have elaborated and clarified what explanation is, and to have done this in a way that relates coherently to fundamental epistemological considerations is a truly remarkable philosophical feat, although of course there are germs of this theory in the history of philosophy, particularly in Kant.

We may add here that the triadic nature of thought, so important to Peirce, is not necessarily lost by showing induction to be a form of abduction. One still has left, in addition to abduction and deduction, the process of judging (party by feeling) and testing (partly by experiment) the given hypothesis. This process of judging hypotheses is sometimes by Peirce thought of as induction. Peirce seems to think that induction in the sense of sample-taking *is* the process of examining experience or the results of experiments. "Induction is the experimental testing of a theory. ... It sets out with a theory and it measures the degree of concordance of that theory with fact." (5.145)

But contrary to this usage of Peirce's, induction is usually understood to be the process of drawing conclusions or generalizations from experience and not the looking to experience with some hypothesis in mind for testing. This only further confirms Peirce's ambiguous and confused use of the term.

D. WHAT KIND OF ABDUCTIONS ARE MEANINGFUL, SIGNIFICANT, ADMISSIBLE?

Peirce's theory of abduction includes a notion which we have so far failed to notice, namely that some abductions, no matter how good they may

---

[19] *Ibid.*, cf. 2.716-17 and 6.612n.1.

appear to be from the point of view of harmonizing all the data, apparently cannot be admitted as *bona fide* abductions. This opens a topic of wide significance, because (1) it is at the heart of Peirce's theory of pragmaticism, and (2) it causes different interpretations of Peirce. It is quite impossible to overestimate the significance of this problem, and this is especially true in view of the battle in modern philosophy between the positivist and metaphysical camps – if we may be permitted a rather large generalization. It is also important because it is possible to conclude that Peirce fought this battle within himself.

The problem arises in two forms which we may state briefly: First, the pragmatic maxim is supposed to serve to clarify difficult notions and ideas. Peirce entitles the article in which the pragmatic maxim appears, "How to Make Our Ideas Clear." Second, the maxim is supposed to be able to show up some concepts as empty and meaningless or in some cases as indistinguishable from some others. Thus a concept like that of silver can be examined from the pragmatic viewpoint with an eye toward displaying its full meaning. But any hypothesis is also itself a *concept*, and can be examined from this same viewpoint, and according to the theory, some hypotheses can be shown to be empty and meaningless, and, thus, no real hypotheses. Whether or not the pragmatic maxim is up to these tasks and if so in what sense and to what degree is the whole problem in embryo. Since it is by all accounts an issue crucial to a fair understanding of the notion of abduction, we shall have to probe it in some detail and make some rather sustained effort to evaluate Peirce's doctrine, the meaning of it as well as its truth.

First, a few general words on the subject of how one ought to go about reading a man like Peirce. Everyone will admit in the abstract that many of the apparent contradictions and conflicts in Peirce's work result not from any feebleness of intellect or memory on his part, nor in most cases from any basic weakness in his philosophy, but rather from his almost incredible depth and many-sidedness, and a genuinely felt sympathy with widely varying viewpoints. But after admitting this in the abstract, many critics succumb to the temptation of ignoring or explaining away those aspects of Peirce's thought they find disagreeable to themselves, and showing how, on Peirce's own principles, he never could seriously have meant those parts of his philosophy, and even if he did, he could not have defended them. Critics who have not Peirce's breadth of approach thus find it difficult to make sense of certain aspects of his system. Different critics find different aspects of the system valuable. "Evidently," as James Feibleman has said, "each of us is going to have his own Peirce." [20] It so hap-

[20] James Feibleman, *An Introduction to Peirce's Philosophy* (New York: Harper

pens that modern tendencies toward positivism have brought out Peirce's empirical side: "the Peirce of Dr. Buchler is a confused thinker who did much useless work in metaphysics, but who had some brilliant logical insights which were altogether unconnected with his other work." [21] But I think it is fair to say that in Peirce's own estimation at least, *no* part of his work was unconnected with the other parts.

Not only has our view of Peirce been somewhat distorted by undue emphasis on his logic and empiricism, but also the school of James and Dewey has taken yet another aspect of Peirce's thought, his pragmatism, and gone on to develop this other side of Peirce. In the case of James and Dewey, of course, they have developed their own systems and do not have the responsibility of a critic to do Peirce's own philosophy justice. They used it as a springboard for their own thought. The only danger is in confusing James' or Dewey's pragmatism with Peirce's .

In this section, now, we wish to examine the implications of Peirce's pragmatic maxim, with emphasis on its relation to abduction and the admissibility of hypotheses. I will confess at the outset that this is undertaken in the hope of showing Peirce to be considerably more consistent on these points than his critics have generally allowed. This is a most important point since, as mentioned above, it has been the subject of a continuing debate ever since the appearance of the *Collected Papers*, in which all sides of Peirce are fairly represented. But, we might add, while we are speaking generally, that perhaps what really needs to be shown is not so much Peirce's consistency on this or that point, as the truthfulness of this rule: namely, that in dealing with a man as wide and deep in his sympathies and approach as Peirce is, one needs always to interpret what he says in the broadest possible sense and never in the narrowest. This will have the effect of eliminating many or most of the apparent conflicts in his philosophy. This is just the opposite procedure from that one should follow in studying a man like Kant, who always used words with a very narrow meaning – and not always the same meaning for the same word.

One formulation of Peirce's maxim is as follows:

Consider what effects, that might conceivably have practical bearings, we conceive the object of our conception to have. Then, our conception of these effects is the whole of our conception of the object. (5.2)

and Brothers, 1946), p. 484. More importantly, it may be that each of us is going to have his own *world!*
  [21] *Ibid.*

No end of trouble and contradictions face the critic who interprets this maxim too narrowly. It just happens in this case that a *strict* interpretation of the maxim – taking each of the words seriously – is in fact wide enough for all of Peirce's purposes (for he gave the maxim a careful formulation), and difficulties arise, not from taking the maxim seriously and literally, but rather from forcibly narrowing its application.

For example, W. B. Gallie claims to find a serious problem in the fact that for any given concept, say the concept of "wine," no one is actually able to list in a strict, scientific and complete sense, *all* of the sensible consequences that are implied in it. Gallie points out that Peirce says many times that the *whole* meaning of a concept is in its possible practical consequences. But, Gallie reasons, if the *whole* meaning of a concept consists in a complete list of its empirical consequences, then the maxim is much too demanding to be of any use in ordinary affairs. Perhaps such a list could be drawn up for rigorously scientific concepts such as silver, or hardness, weight and force. But even the most common notions such as that of wine defy rigorous treatment.

We may therefore conclude that if Pragmatism, in its narrower form, were to be applied to most of our everyday, as opposed to our scientific, conceptions of different kinds of substance, nothing but useless pedantry would result.[22]

Gallie gives this thought considerable development, showing in several examples what he means and how Peirce's maxim fails. He discusses wine, time, the detective and his murder case, and the jar of alcohol on the laboratory shelf and how its continued existence is periled by the charwoman and the lab boy, all of which cases are designed to show the futility of applying Peirce's maxim to anything but technical scientific notions.

In all of this Gallie is fighting nothing but a straw man – a creation of his own narrow reading of Peirce's maxim. The pragmatic maxim does in fact say that the meaning of a notion consists in all its conceivable practical consequences: but it does not say or even imply that *all* of these practical consequences have to be spelled out thoroughly and rigorously before the concept has any meaning at all. What the maxim does imply is that *enough* of these consequences must be spelled out in order, first, to insure that the concept has sense, that is, can be tied down to the world of possible sensible effects, and, second, to insure that the concept can be distinguished from other similar concepts. In other words the pragmatic maxim first, proves that a concept is not empty if it can be tied down to conceivable practical effects, and, second, brings out the concept's dis-

[22] Gallie, *op. cit.*, p. 168.

tinguishing features. The maxim clears up hard words. Peirce never says that *every* possible consequence must be listed in order to have a significant concept. Of course, if *every* practical effect could be enumerated that would indeed constitute the *entire* meaning of the concept – but this is an ideal, and I doubt that Peirce believed that it ever could be perfectly fulfilled in the case even of the most rigorous scientific term because every term whatever has a certain penumbra of vagueness, and if not the term itself, then the terms used to explicate it. In fact, who can doubt that to spell out *all* the possible empirical consequences of an hypothesis or of a word like "silver" would be as pedantic in science as a similar treatment of the word "wine" would be in everyday life? The nearest Peirce ever comes to supporting this interpretation of Gallie's is where he says: "*Retroduction* [abduction] is the provisional adoption of a hypothesis because every possible consequence of it is capable of experimental verification ...." (1.68, my brackets) But the point even here is not that "every possible consequence" *must be tested,* but merely must be *capable* of being tested (but not necessarily tested *directly!* *Cf.* 2.642f., and 5.597 and 599) [23] Peirce says that *all* the operations of chemistry have failed (in his day!) to decompose hydrogen, but there is *a priori* reason to doubt that all *possible* operations of chemistry have been tried on this element or any other.

In another place, Peirce says that hypotheses should be "tested by experiment *so far as practicable.*" (6.524, my emph.) Wennerberg says, "W. B. Gallie has, I think, misunderstood the import of the pragmatic maxim." [24] He supports this conclusion with considerations similar to the ones I have offered above.

Gallie is aware that his narrow interpretation of the maxim is not the only possible one, and gives a wider interpretation, which coincides exactly with what I would say is the *only* reasonable interpretation of the maxim.[25] There is no justification for his narrow interpretation. All of Peirce's references to the fact that the *sum* of the practical consequences gives us the meaning of a notion do not constitute an imperative for us actually to list all of them, but only express an ideal. The spirit and letter of the maxim are completely fulfilled when *enough* consequences are listed to show the concept to be different from other concepts and to show it to be a non-empty concept.

This brings the discussion to a much more important misunderstanding of the pragmatic maxim – a misunderstanding not limited to Gallie but

---

[23] Compare also Hjalmar Wennerberg, *The Pragmatism of C. S. Peirce* (Copenhagen: Bjnar Munksgaard, 1962), pp. 133f.
[24] *Ibid.,* pp. 134f.
[25] See Gallie, *op. cit.,* pp. 170f.

including almost all critics with an empirical leaning. In a word, this misunderstanding consists in the idea that by all rights the pragmatic maxim ought to exclude metaphysical propositions of any kind from having meaning or admissibility as explanatory hypotheses. In this case it is possible to see some ground for the misunderstanding, but even in order to do this the maxim must be interpreted very narrowly indeed, and it is all but obvious that Peirce himself never meant the maxim to be used in this fashion.

We have already given some attention to the problem of what Peirce meant by hypothesis and abduction, and we will also need to study some of the specific applications Peirce himself gave of his maxim to metaphysical notions. Only in this way can a fair estimation be gained of Peirce's real intention in his maxim.

Let us now consider the relationship between Pragmatism and the logic of abduction. Peirce fully realized the difficulties involved in justifying induction and abduction as forms of argument. And he was perfectly serious when he suggested that the theory that each true induction is a miracle directly inspired by God was worthy of some respect. I suppose he did not believe it, but he did point out that as a solution it recognized the difficulty in its fullness, and tied its answer to an ultimate view of the universe. (2.690) His own justification of induction rests partly on his belief that man's mind has a kinship with nature, and partly upon the nature of induction itself (see 5.591f.), and partly on his realism. The matter hangs together organically.

Now, Peirce considered that his philosophy was a carefully integrated whole, and especially he thought of his pragmatic maxim as in close connection with his theory of hypothesis.

If you carefully consider the question of pragmatism you will see that it is nothing else than the question of the logic of abduction. That is, pragmatism proposes a certain maxim which, if sound, must render needless any further rule as to the admissibility of hypotheses to rank as hypotheses, that is to say, as explanations of phenomena held as hopeful suggestions; and, furthermore, this is all that the maxim of pragmatism really pretends to do, at least so far as it is confined to logic, and is not understood as a proposition of psychology. (5.196)

This is a key sentence in that it has afforded encouragement to those who incline to find a modified positivism in Peirce – although to find such encouragement one has to overlook the context and in particular the last sentence of this very paragraph (see below).

Peirce anticipated that his maxim would be taken as if it were another formulation of the positivism of Comte and Poincare, and was at pains to deny any connection between his maxim and their position. (2.511n, and 5.198) Comte's positivism, as Peirce understood it, ruled out any hypothesis that could not be *directly* tested. Pushing this rule to its extreme, as Peirce rightly said was our duty, shows that nothing can be known about history – which is absurd. Nor does it permit predictions. Peirce has therefore ruled out at least the stark forms of positivism as being the correct interpretation of his maxim.

Kant, in his first *Critique,* had a good deal to say on the subject of hypotheses. It might be thought that there would be some similarity between Kant and Peirce on this point considering Peirce's long study of Kant and also because of certain remarks Peirce every so often scatters throughout his writings, such as "Kant (whom I *more* than admire) is nothing but a somewhat confused pragmatist." (5.525)

Kant gives extended treatment to the notion of hypothesis in his appendix to the Transcendental Dialectic, "The Regulative Employment of the Ideas of Pure Reason." [26] In this section Kant argues that in spite of the fact that reason is led by various teleological connections in the world to form the idea of a creator God, such an idea cannot be called a true hypothesis because it has to do with no object of possible experience. The idea, strictly speaking, is empty. Nevertheless, the idea, if held critically, may serve as a principle to regulate empirical inquiry. A genuine hypothesis for Kant had to deal with an object of possible experience. Thus the scientific hypothesis that there existed "antediluvian monsters" was legitimate (although this quite overlooks the difficulty of finding the sense in which the past is subject to possible experience.) It is evident from this brief statement of Kant's view that there is here a strong streak of the positivism Peirce deplored in Comte, and that Kant's view, though somewhat closer to Peirce, is not identical with Peirce's view. This will be somewhat more clearly seen below.

There is, however, a possibility of bringing the two men closer together. According to Peirce's maxim, we must ask, "What practical consequences does the idea of a creator God lead to?" Answer (from Kant): "It leads us to investigate the world *as if* it were the product of intelligent creation." This, then, is the actual meaning of the word "God" according to the maxim. In this sense it is not an empty concept, but there is nothing in this approach to offend Kant. Kant said, of course, a great deal about God that we are ignoring here, and I only mention this as an interesting line

[26] Immanuel Kant, *Critique of Pure Reason,* Trans. Norman Kemp Smith (New York: Macmillan & Co., 1961), pp. 532-570.

of thought that perhaps warrants fuller treatment. It will become clearer below that the gulf between Kant and Peirce is very wide and probably could not really be bridged by the line of thought indicated here.

Just what did Peirce mean by his pragmatic maxim, and what did he mean to exclude by it? Peirce goes some way toward answering these questions in these two sentences: "Suffice it to say once more that pragmatism is, in itself, no doctrine of metaphysics, no attempt to determine any truth of things. It is merely a method of ascertaining the meanings of hard words and of abstract concepts." (5.464) The fact that "in itself" the maxim teaches no doctrine of metaphysics shows again Peirce's desire to avoid positivism. Pragmatism of itself solves no real problem.[27] More to the point perhaps is this unambiguous statement:

For my part, I cannot admit the proposition of Kant – that there are certain impassable bounds to human knowledge; and, even if there are such bounds in regard to the infinite and absolute, the question of future life, as distinct from the question of immortality, does not transcend them. (6.556)

Interestingly enough, in support of this thesis he points to Comte's prediction that man would never be able to determine the chemical constitution of the stars.

And finally, in all fairness to those who interpret the maxim more strictly than I think necessary, it must be acknowledged that there are places where Peirce himself seems to give it a narrow interpretation (especially in 1.68, quoted above), and particularly the way in a later article he seems to back away from too narrow an interpretation of the maxim – implying that even if he never committed himself in words to too radical an application of the maxim he nevertheless felt an impulse later on to put it in a broader perspective. This occurs in an article of 1902 where he said that the maxim was "only a step" in his fuller philosophy of synechism. And he pointed out that after an idea had been purified by an application of the maxim,

a still higher grade of clearness of thought can be attained by remembering that the only ultimate good which the practical facts to which it directs attention can subserve is to further the development of concrete reasonableness; so that the meaning of the concept does not lie in any individual reactions at all, but in the manner in which those reactions contribute to that development. (5.3)

But even here he has not in the least abandoned the maxim, but rather called for a wide understanding of it.

[27] See Feibleman, op. cit., p. 297. Of course, Comte or Ayer would say as much of their own maxims.

Now in exactly what sense are we to understand Peirce when he says that the maxim determines the fitness of an hypothesis to be entertained? The best way to answer that is to examine several cases where Peirce applied the maxim and see how he himself used it. For a maxim so important in Peirce's system, he proved somewhat bashful about applying it to specific cases, and especially to those extreme cases in which we are so extraordinarily interested. Nevertheless, there are, among others, applications of the maxim to the concepts of time, substance, and hardness. There are in addition hints as to how the maxim should be applied to the idea of God. For further illustrative purposes I will apply it to the idea of absolute motion.

1.   Time

Peirce's application of the pragmatic maxim to the concept of time (5.458*ff.*) is perhaps somewhat cursory, but I would not want to associate myself with Gallie's judgment that it is "surely simple-minded to a degree." [28] That remark presupposes that someone else has had more success in rendering clear our idea of time than Peirce had. There is no consensus to this effect.

To be brief, Peirce finds the "practical" meaning of time to be something on this order: the past represents those events over which we have no control; the future, those over which we have a measure of control; and the present, those which we are endeavoring to control. He is perhaps weakest in his formulation of the idea of the present, as he has rightly said, "As for the Present instant, it is so inscrutable that I wonder whether no sceptic has ever attacked its reality." (5.459) This, as I say, is cursory, but it does fulfill to a sufficient degree the requirements of the maxim to show that time is not a meaningless concept and that the concept of the past, for example, can be "practically" distinguished from that of the future. This analysis is not as thorough perhaps as it could be, but it is at least a step on the way to clarifying a hard word indeed and should not be dismissed. It is a good example of the way Peirce intended his maxim to be used.

2.   Hardness

Much of what can be said of the concept of "time" applies equally to the concept of "hardness." These are abstract ideas which cannot be dismissed

[28] Gallie, *op. cit.*, p. 169.

as ultimately irreducible notions. Abstract ideas, along with every other idea, must "give account of themselves," in the words of Peirce's editors.[29]

A diamond may be said to be hard, because what is meant by "hard" is, pragmatically, the ability to resist being scratched by many substances. A diamond that burned up before anyone had a chance to scratch it, can be said to be hard because it "would have" resisted scratching:

> For to what else does the entire teaching of chemistry relate except to the "behavior" of different possible kinds of material substance? And in what does that behavior consist except that if a substance of a certain kind should be exposed to an agency of a certain kind, a certain kind of sensible result *would* ensue, according to our experience hitherto. As for the pragmaticist, it is precisely his position that nothing else than this can be so much as *meant* by saying that an object possesses a character. (5.457)

3. Eucharist

The cases so far considered are rather straightforward applications of the maxim. However, Peirce's analysis of the notion of substance is an instance of going to an extreme case to set his doctrine in clearer relief. Peirce takes the instance of the Catholic-Protestant controversy over the Eucharist. The Catholics maintain that the bread and wine are transformed or transubstantiated into the literal body and blood of Christ. They acknowledge that the elements retain the "accidents" of bread and wine, but contend that in their "substance" they are flesh and blood. In Peirce's estimation this is a fine example of a sham battle, and his reasons for so believing should be evident. But then he adds a mysterious closing sentence: "It is foolish for Catholics and Protestants to fancy themselves in disagreement about the elements of the sacrament, if they agree in regard to all their sensible effects, here and hereafter." (5.401)

How seriously he meant this I do not know, but if we assume he meant it seriously, it shows how very, very broadly he understood his pragmatic maxim. Consider the implications of the idea of "sensible effects *hereafter.*" Well, the pragmatic maxim quite explicitly says that our idea of a thing consists in all its *conceivable* sensible effects.

I would not want to rest a great deal on this case alone, but the simple truth is that Peirce continually applies his maxim to just such extraordinary and "metaphysical" notions, and these applications more than anything else explain his real intention in the maxim. What he says about the hypothesis of God will, I am confident, confirm this point.

[29] 5.v and see 5.207.

On this point it is well to observe that in a late (1902) essay, *Reason's Rules*, Peirce seems to reject his earlier treatment of the problem of transubstantiation. He says that the difference between the Catholic and Protestant views *is real* and consists in different future expectations:

> The implication is that the layman may sometime know, presumably will, in another world; and that he may *expect* that if he ever does come to know, he will find the priest to be right. Thus, analysis shows that even in regard to so excessively metaphysical a matter, the belief, if there can be any belief, has to involve expectation as its very essence. (5.541)

The Protestant and Catholic thus have different expectations about what the future will reveal on this question and presumably one may say from this that their beliefs differ.

4. *Absolute and relative motion*

Before considering the relation of the pragmatic maxim to the idea of God, I will take the opportunity here to examine the notion of absolute motion. Newton held that space and motion were absolute. By this he meant that even if there were only one object in the universe, it might significantly be said to move. Berkeley held the contrary view. Movement, he said, was nothing but change of distance between one body *and another*. Thus, if there were only one body in all of space, it could not be said to move, for there would be nothing relative to which it could move. This is an interesting argument, for Newton and Berkeley would agree that there are no practical differences between each other's hypotheses: that is, no sensible difference can be detected whichever hypothesis one adopts. At this point in the discussion, one is tempted to say that under Peirce's maxim there is no difference between the hypothesis of relative and absolute motion. But now Newton comes forward with a suggestion worthy of his genius. Consider, says Newton, the case of circular motion. Suppose the one object in the universe is a contrivance of two heavy weights connected with a rope of some length. True enough, there is no other object in the universe relative to which one can say that this contrivance is moving. But if one arranges a spring-scale to measure the tension in the rope, one can tell if the apparatus is spinning. If the apparatus is not spinning, no tension will be registered in the rope; but if the apparatus is spinning, centrifugal force will pull on the rope. Thus, one can tell if there is motion even if there were only one thing in the universe.[30]

---

[30] See Isaac Newton, "Absolute and Relative Space, Time, and Motion," and George Berkeley, "Criticism of Newton's Doctrines on Space," in Arthur Danto and Sidney

Clearly the experiment never can be tried. But, "consider what effects, that might *conceivably* have practical bearings . . . ." Newton's experiment is a thought experiment and can be nothing else. Yet he has shown in some sense a *conceivable* difference between his hypothesis and that of Berkeley, and no one can avoid at least feeling that he has clarified what we mean by these two "hard words." This is a wonderful case of clearing up to some degree a very hazy and confused difference between notions by following Peirce's injunction: that is, thinking of some conceivable practical difference between notions. One is constrained to believe that in some way or another Peirce has made a real contribution to philosophy at this point.

(Incidentally, Peirce knew of the absolute-relative motion controversy and sided with Newton. In 7.484*ff.* he examines Mach's modern arguments against Newton's view and gives them a pretty sound trouncing. Murphey, in his brief discussion, labors under the impression that Einstein's theories have served to refute Newton's views,[31] but I do not know how relativity theory has this implication, and doubt, in fact, that it does.)

E. THE HYPOTHESIS OF GOD: A TEST CASE

Peirce's treatment of the problem of theism "may be taken as an illustration of his metaphysical method stretched to its limits," says Manley Thompson. Peirce in 1905 stated clearly that his maxim would show that "almost" every proposition of "ontological metaphysics" was either gibberish or absurd. This, he said, made his philosophy a kind of "propepositivism" – but differing from positivism in three regards: (1) it retains the "precious essence" from metaphysics, (2) its "full acceptance of the main body of our instinctive beliefs," and (3) its insistence on scholastic realism. (5.423) Even in such a passage as this, designed on the surface to put alarm into the metaphysicians, there is really very little positivism left after all the qualifications are made. Peirce's realism is certainly a highly metaphysical doctrine.

I wish to linger for a while over the problem of God's existence and discuss it in some detail, first, because what Peirce says on the subject is vastly interesting; second, because, as Manley Thompson indicates, it is an extreme case of Peirce's theories on abduction and the admissibility of

Morgenbesser (edd.), *Philosophy of Science* (New York: The World Publishing Co., 1960), pp. 322-335. One may very well raise the question: Is this contrivance described above "one thing"? If not, since it has parts, what would "one thing" be?
[31] Murphey, *op. cit.*, p. 382.

hypotheses, and the results of this test case are very enlightening, and third, because it is in its own right one of the major problems of philosophy. But the second reason is paramount. A great number of Peirce's most illuminating remarks on his theory of abduction are made in the context of his discussion of God. Wennerberg says, "In *A Neglected Argument for the Reality of God* Peirce has given his *best* presentation of how he thinks that an inquiry in accordance with the scientific method ought to be performed." [32]

Long ago Kant observed that the problems of God, freedom, and immortality are the metaphysical questions *par excellence*. This is true in all three cases partly because of the vital bearing these problems have on all human life and conduct. These are not differences which make no difference. Other speculative questions such as, what constitutes a "relation," or an "event," are very interesting, no doubt, and, in so far as the whole of reality is interconnected, have a bearing on all speculative questions; but they are, or at least seem to be, far removed from the real problems of human life, in a way that the problems of God, freedom, and immortality are not. But there is more justification for calling these the metaphysical questions *par excellence,* than their bearing on human interests alone. For they also cut through virtually all other questions in such a way that if they were solved many other major questions would fall into place, at least in general outline. This is particularly true in the case of the problem of the existence and nature of God. This is the problem of all problems both in a theoretical and a practical sense. There are few philosophical systems, if any, which do not find in this *the* crucial issue, although it is sometimes fashionable to feign indifference to the question. This indifference mostly takes the form of an unstated presupposition that *either* it is so clear that God exists that argument is not called for to support the point, some even saying that such arguments are blasphemous, and others feeling in their hearts that unbelievers may only be considered wholly perverse and wicked, *or,* on the other hand, that all modern thought has long since acknowledged that "God is dead" and it would be a waste of time to belabor this ancient superstition. But in fact, the question, in one form or another, has agitated thinkers ever since the time of the pre-Socratics and is likely to continue to do so into the indefinite future. But in any case it is preposterous to act as if the question made no philosophical difference.

In Peirce's famous essay titled, "A Neglected Argument for the Reality of God," he begins with a summary outline of his whole philosophical

---

[32] Wennerberg, *op. cit.*, p. 169. My emph.

system, especially the categories. This resume was certainly necessary if he was ever to hope to make his considerations on the subject of theism at all intelligible, much less persuasive, to his readers. After this resume he then expresses his opinion that if there is a benign God, there ought to be an argument for His existence "obvious to all minds, high and low alike." (6.457) And not a mere abstract argument, but one "applicable to the conduct of life." This brings to mind Hume's amused comments at the opening of his section on Scepticism in his *Enquiry*: How is it, Hume wonders, that the theologians on the one hand debate whether any man can be so blind as to be an atheist, and on the other busy themselves trying to devise proofs of God's existence? [33] But it is not at all inconceivable that the theologians are faced with the problem of making clear to confused minds what in itself is clear and obvious in the extreme – this at least is the way Peirce conceives his problem. He says, *in this context,* that ". . . facts that stand before our face and eyes and stare us in the face are far from being, in all cases, the ones most easily discerned." (6.162)

Peirce's main approach to God is through what he impishly calls "musement." What he means by this is a kind of mental play:

I have often occasion to walk at night, for about a mile, over an entirely untravelled road, much of it between open fields without a house in sight. The circumstances are not favorable to severe study, but are so to calm meditation. If the sky is clear, I look at the stars in the silence, thinking how each successive increase in the aperture of a telescope makes many more of them visible than all that had been visible before. The fact that the heavens do not show a sheet of light proves that there are vastly more dark bodies, say planets, than there are suns. They must be inhabited, and most likely millions of them with beings much more intelligent than we are. For on the whole, the solar system seems one of the simplest; and presumably under more complicated phenomena greater intellectual power will be developed. What must be the social phenomena of such a world! How extraordinary are the minds even of the lower animals. We cannot appreciate our own powers any more than a writer can appreciate his own style, or a thinker the peculiar quality of his own thought. . . . Let a man drink in such thoughts as come to him in contemplating the physico-psychical universe without any special purpose of his own; especially the universe of mind which coincides with the universe of matter. The idea of there being a God over it all of course will be often suggested; and the more he considers it, the more he will be enwrapt with Love of this idea. He will ask himself whether or not there really is a God. If he allows instinct to speak, and searches his own heart, he will at length find that he cannot help believing it. I cannot tell how every

[33] David Hume, "An Enquiry Concerning Human Understanding," *The English Philosophers From Bacon to Mill,* Edwin A. Burtt, ed. (N.Y.: The Modern Library, 1939), p. 679.

man will think. I know the majority of men, especially men, are so full of pedantries – especially the male sex – that they cannot think straight about these things. But I can tell how a man must think if he is a pragmatist. (6.501)

Peirce elaborates on musement, saying that he does not mean by it what we would call reverie – an aimless, imbecilic wandering of the mind. But rather a more or less careful thought, lacking only a *determined* direction or purpose. Peirce likens it to play where one has "a lively exercise of one's powers." (6.1458) A reverie would have too little discipline – like playing tennis without a net.

He points out that it would not be scientific to sit down with the purpose of persuading oneself of God's existence, and, moreover, one would always suspect oneself of not reasoning fairly. One might say something here about the charge that is often leveled against theists, and to which Peirce might be considered open. And that is that our reasonings are or may be (Freud was confident enough for the former expression) the illegitimate fruit of our *unconscious* desire to believe. This charge must be entirely dismissed as positively valueless and that for two irrefutable reasons. (1) The charge may with equal propriety be leveled against those of a contrary opinion, or against anyone with any opinion at all, at least if some kind of plausible explanation accompanies it, and it thus nullifies itself. The charge implicitly denies the power of reason, and thus undercuts all rational discourse whatever, including whatever considerations may have been thought to lead to it itself. (2) No man can do anything more than reason honestly. If he permits *conscious* predilections to have weight with his reasonings, this will perhaps be dishonest. (On the use of the word "perhaps" here, see the next paragraph). He can only hope that no illegitimate longings have slipped into his line of thought. If they have, he is still powerless to do anything about them, for being *unconscious* of them, his position is hopeless. And the same applies to any man and any man's position whatever.

But, in this regard, we may anticipate a later chapter enough to point out that it is a cornerstone of Peirce's philosophy that human instincts, so far as they bear on judgment as well as on action are far from pernicious in their influence, but positively helpful. Freud's position that all men have a natural longing to believe in God is taken as true by Peirce, and not used of itself as a proof for God as inferior thinkers have been wont to do, but used as a hint or indication – a hint supported and given validity by the wider context of his whole philosophy of science which proposes to explain how the mind comes to any truth whatever. But this is not surprising, since

Freud's approach was a kind of determinism and materialism, and opposed in almost every particular to Peirce's view of the world.

It is interesting again to observe the circularity involved in Freud's view and in Peirce's as well, and the difference between them.

But let us return to the idea of "musement." The mind must be given free reign when searching for an explanatory hypothesis. Creative leaps are notoriously unpredictable and usually cannot be forced. In the case of God, however, the hypothesis has already been suggested, in that most people have heard talk of God from their earliest years. What Peirce is evidently trying to do is to get people to "rediscover" the hypothesis on their own, so that they will be able to see for themselves and from the "inside" what a magnificent hypothesis it is, how beautifully it serves to interconnect all phenomena. And people, when they see this for themselves, will hopefully experience the same thrill of discovery and inner conviction of certainly that accompanies almost all important creative steps, whether they be in science, mathematics, music, or whatever, even when these steps are merely being retraced by the thinker. As has already been pointed out, and as Peirce would be among the first to acknowledge, this instinctive and powerful feeling of certainty is no infallible guide – although as Poincare points out in his brilliant essay on creativity,[34] such a feeling rarely if ever accompanies an hypothesis which would not have been beautiful and fitting and appropriate in at least a limited regard – even if it is a false hypothesis. But Peirce does not feel that the hypothesis of God stands anything to lose by reflection made upon it in a cool moment, when the flush of "discovery" or "re-discovery" has passed. On the contrary, he holds that the hypothesis grows in power and beauty the more it is reflected upon. He believes that the hypothesis "will find response in every part of [man's] mind," (6.465) and consequently the hypothesis grows in power the more it is examined from every different perspective.

But there are several points that need to be cleared up. First, people who are accustomed to a certain kind of highly rigorous thought, perhaps scientists and mathematicians in general, will be inclined to object that this "musement" is nothing in the world except a funny name for sloppy thinking – or if not "sloppy thinking" exactly, then at least speculation of a very uncontrolled kind, speculation that might conceivably lead to any kind of guess which might strike one as clever and powerful. This charge has a good deal of truth in it from a certain viewpoint, but it is the

[34] See "Mathematical Creation," in *The Creative Process*, B. Ghiselin, ed. (N.Y.: The New American Library, 1955).

viewpoint which badly needs correcting. Peirce observes that the kind of "free-thinking" he is encouraging in the process of musement (is this what free-thinking has come to!) is precisely the kind of thought which is used in all significant discovery of matters of fact. To look toward the kind of rigid, controlled thought one finds in deductive mathematics is again to commit that fallacy which underlies so much modern philosophy and which has already been explicated in some detail. But Peirce allows there is a second reason why people will suspect musement, and perhaps to a lesser extent, will suspect everything he has said on the wider subject of abduction and instinct, and that is that people who have used that kind of thought, particularly the philosophers, have been so *dogmatic* as regards their conclusions, which, of course, never agree. But dogmatism is at bottom the same kind of sin the "mathematical" philosophers make: the belief, or, only slightly better, the hope, that one's conclusions are demonstrable or certain. It is, then, equally a mistake for the muser to become dogmatic as it is for the "tough-thinker," as he fancies himself, to scoff at musement on principle.

But there is another point which profitably can be raised in connection with musement, and that is, what kind of thought does Peirce have in mind *exactly*? Well, of course, it is part of the point of musement that one cannot answer that question "exactly," since the muser is supposed to come to the hypothesis by his own path so that he will feel the force of the discovery to the full extent. But any path will suffice, in Peirce's view. The doctrine of God finds "response in every part of the mind" so the effect is the same whether one contemplates beauty, morality, life, physics, psychology, or philosophy in general. The only limitation is that one must not undertake a too vigorous logical analysis, first, because the subject of God, of all possible subjects, is most vague and unsuited to premature efforts toward exactitude, and, second, because logical analysis is no way to make creative discoveries, but rather one is supposed to go on *"automatic control"* (6.462) in this experiment!

But on the question of what line musement will take, Peirce at least has given us samples taken from his own experience. For example, the things described in the above quotation where he described the process of musement. Another sample is found later: "In growth, too, we find that the three Universes *conspire*; and a universal feature of it is provision for later stages in earlier ones. This is a specimen of certain lines of reflection which will inevitably suggest the hypothesis of God's reality." (6.465)

This argument mentioned here (the "provision for later stages in earlier ones") is a somewhat more subtle point than might at first appear. It is, in fact, the same point which seems to have been responsible for setting Bergson off on the construction of his very provocative evolutionary philosophy – not, be it noted, a *naturalistic* or *mechanistic* theory of evolution at all, but rather an evolution involving a highly occult power which works in a way quite beyond the power of the human mind to fathom. It was this very phenomenon of uncanny "conspiracy," as Peirce calls it, which was the key to Bergson's theory, particularly the "conspiracy" that seems to be involved in the rise of highly complex organs and instincts which have these two features: (1) The whole life cycle of the organism depends upon them, and (2) An intermediate stage of development cannot be imagined. Such things as the web-spinning mechanism of the spider, the origin of wings in reptiles, birds, mammals, and insects, the instinct and organs for the building of functional wax cells in the case of the honey bee, and the phenomenon of metamorphosis – and sometimes even a double or triple metamorphosis – such phenomena as these are meant. If indeed there is a kind of teleological "conspiracy" involved here, that will certainly make some people look on the hypothesis of God with some favor.

Peirce claims to have three arguments for the reality of God, but these are interconnected into something of an unclear tangle. The fact that musement leads one to God is his chief argument, and he calls it the "Humble Argument." He alleges that not only is musement the most powerful argument for God, but also it is the best argument since it does not depend upon rigorous analysis nor upon long formal education. In fact the argument takes its best form in the mind of the "clodhopper" – whence its name. (6.483) Nothing is more inimical to the argument than a little education which, when it is broad, puffs a man up, giving him the feeling he has discovered or perhaps even created all the truths he has lately learned, while he does nothing but accept uncritically every new wind of doctrine, and, when it is narrow, makes him feel that his competence in his specialty gives importance to whatever other opinions he may happen to hold.

This musement, then, is the humble argument. The "neglected" argument "consists in showing that the humble argument is the natural fruit of free meditation, since every heart will be ravished by the beauty and adorability of the Idea, when it is so pursued" (6.487) And the third argument, the one most relevant to our over-all purpose, is the study of "logical methodeutic" (6.488) which justifies the other two arguments philosophically. Peirce even goes so far as to say, in a later discussion of this third argument, that if his theory concerning the nature of human thinking is proved, then so is God's reality, so closely does that hypothesis follow from the epistemological foundation. (6.491) This is an amazing claim!

It is surely clear that Peirce's "proofs" of God's reality are only probable in nature, as is the case for any proposition concerning matters of fact: he speaks of this "strictly hypothetical God." (6.467) For Peirce, as we understand, any matter of existence, including the self and the outside world, is an hypothesis. So although God is strictly hypothetical, He is known on the same ground as everything else: by abduction. Whether one agrees with Peirce or not on the question of theism, it appears to me that Peirce is absolutely right in pointing to the notion that God is an hypothesis as much as any other matter of fact, an hypothesis arrived at by the same process as any other and to be judged by the same criteria: aesthetic or intuitive appeal, explanatory power, and agreement with other facts in so far as they are known.

This approach seems to me to be in conformity with the judgment of common sense. The ordinary man is not usually of the opinion that God's existence can be *proved* in the mathematical sense (what would be the room for faith?), nor does he ordinarily think that the idea of God is not even a legitimate speculation, as the positivists would have it. Thus Peirce justifies yet again his description of his philosophy as "critical common-sensism." In fact a good argument could be made that all of the main results of supposing all human knowledge to be inferential in nature are in conformity with common sense – perhaps with a minimum of explanation. This, if true, would have been important to Peirce, since he was persuaded that most of our "everyday" notions are practically indubitable and it is useless to try to persuade ourselves otherwise on philosophical or rational grounds. Hume, of course, admitted as much.

If believers in the deductive perfection of the ontological argument ever have moments when they doubt God's existence, that shows they really don't *believe* the argument fully. *Full* belief *acts* like full belief all the time: i.e., never doubts. Likewise, if positivists ever, in the privacy of their chambers, suspect God's existence, it shows they really do not believe fully that He is not a real hypothesis. They make the possibility of positivism's falsehood a real hypothesis. Perhaps one of the earliest statements of the pragmatic doctrine of belief was given in the Book of James: "Belief without works is dead." Critical common-sensism allows both believers and non-believers to doubt – without betraying their intellectual principles. For Peirce, nothing, under the right circumstances, is theoretically immune from doubt (a corollary of fallibilism), but many things are practically immune.

In the following quotation Peirce elaborates on the nature of a "simple," "natural," and "facile" theory, all in the context of the Neglected Argument. His last sentence is very revealing.

Modern science has been builded after the model of Galileo, who founded it, on *il lume naturale*. That truly inspired prophet had said that, of two hypotheses, the *simpler* is to be preferred; but I was formerly one of those who, in our dull self-conceit fancying ourselves more sly than he, twisted the maxim to mean the *logically* simpler, the one that adds the least to what has been observed, in spite of three obvious objections: first, that so there was no support for any hypothesis; secondly, that by the same token we ought to content ourselves with simply formulating the special observations actually made; and thirdly, that every advance of science that further opens the truth to our view discloses a world of unexpected complications. It was not until long experience forced me to realize that subsequent discoveries were every time showing I had been wrong, while those who understood the maxim as Galileo had done, early unlocked the secret, that the scales fell from my eyes and my mind awoke to the broad and flaming daylight that it is the simpler Hypothesis in the sense of the more facile and natural, the one that instinct suggests, that must be preferred; for the reason that, unless man have a natural bent in accordance with nature's, he has no chance of understanding nature at all. Many tests of this principal and positive fact, relating as well to my own studies as to the researches of others, have confirmed me in this opinion; and when I shall come to set them forth in a book, their array will convince everybody. On, no! I am forgetting that armour, impenetrable by accurate thought, in which the rank and file of minds are clad! They may, for example, get the notion that my proposition involves a denial of the rigidity of the laws of association: it would be quite on a par with much that is current. I do not mean that logical simplicity is a consideration of no value at all, but only that its value is badly secondary to that of simplicity in the other sense.

If, however, the maxim is correct in Galileo's sense, whence it follows that man has, in some degree, a divinatory power, primary or derived, like that of a wasp or a bird, then instances swarm to show that a certain altogether peculiar confidence in a hypothesis, not to be confounded with rash cocksureness, has a very appreciable value as a sign of the truth of the hypothesis. I regret I cannot give an account of certain interesting and almost convincing cases. The N.A. excites this peculiar confidence in the very highest degree. (6.477)

It might be possible to agree with Peirce's theory that all knowledge is abductive in nature, and that all creative leaps are abductive, while at the same time holding that there is a vast difference between the inference, say, that other personalities exist, and the theory that God exists. Just to take one consideration, one might allege that the evidence of the senses is almost conclusive on the first point, but at best doubtful on the second. This might be an important consideration if the question were merely whether there are other human *bodies* in the world, but the point is not applicable to the question, are there other *feeling centers* or *personalities* (or "souls" if you prefer) in the world. On this question all the sensory evidence is so far quite indirect and the leap of inference is based—on what? Partly on the evidence of the *heart,* if Peirce's lead may be followed. Peirce says:

> We can know nothing except what we directly experience. So all that we can anyway know relates to experience. All the creations of our mind are but patchworks from experience. So that all our ideas are but ideas of real or transposed experience. A word can mean nothing except the idea it calls up. So that we cannot even *talk* about anything but a knowable object. The unknowable about which Hamilton and the agnostics talk can be nothing but an Unknowable Knowable. The absolutely unknowable is a nonexistence. The Unknowable is a nominalistic heresy. (6.492)
>
> Where would such an idea, say as that of God, come from if not from direct experience? Would you make it a result of some kind of reasoning, good or bad? Why, reasoning can supply the mind with nothing in the world except an estimate of the value of a statistical ratio, that is, how often certain kinds of things are found in certain combinations in the ordinary course of experience. And scepticism in the sense of doubt of the validity of elementary ideas – which is really a proposal to turn the idea out of court and permit no inquiry into its applicability – is doubly condemned by the fundamental principle of scientific method – condemned first as obstructing inquiry, and condemned second because it is treating some other than a statistical ratio as a thing to be argued about. No: as to God, open your eyes – and your heart, which is also a perceptive organ – and you see him. But you may ask, Don't you admit there are any delusions? Yes: I may think a thing is black, and on close examination it may turn out to be bottle-green. But I cannot think a thing is black if there is no such thing to be seen as black. Neither can I think that a certain action is self-sacrificing, if no such thing as self-sacrifice exists, although it may be very rare. It is the nominalists, and the nominalists alone, who indulge in such scepticism, which the scientific method utterly condemns. (6.493)

Peirce here opens up another gold mine of suggestion. Can one deny that the "heart" is a sensitive organ? What does this mean, anyway? That a man's whole being – rational, emotional, instinctive, – may feel a tug toward – toward what? ideas? people? both? more besides? Surely it is at least a minimal part of Peirce's meaning here that one must "open one's heart" to the idea of God, perhaps in much the same way that one may consciously "open one's heart" to a beggar or to someone in distress (these comparisons may not be fortunate). *One must let the idea come under favorable scrutiny, one must nurture it and let it grow if it will, play with it and see how it would affect one's life and thought.* This is a test of an hypothesis! [35] This is nothing more than the nominalist does with his idea or anyone does with an idea he has come upon more or less originally. Peirce believes that the *absolute* sterility of nominalism as a way of looking at the world will not permit it to withstand "open-hearted" comparison with realism, and, as a corollary, theism, for much longer than an hour or two.

But there is another passage which bears upon these points that is so rich in suggestion that it cannot be passed over:

If a pragmaticist is asked what he means by the word "God," he can only say that just as long acquaintance with a man of great character may deeply influence one's whole manner of conduct, so that a glance at his portrait may make a difference, just as almost living Dr. Johnson enabled poor Boswell to write an immortal book and a really sublime book, just as long study of the works of Aristotle may make him an acquaintance, so if contemplation and study of the physico-psychical universe can imbue a man with principles of conduct analogous to the influence of a great man's works or conversation, then that analogue of a mind – for it is impossible to say that *any* human attribute is *literally* applicable – is what he means by "God." Of course, various great theologians explain that one cannot attribute *reason* to God, nor perception (which always involves an element of surprise and of learning what one did not know), and, in short, that his "mind" is necessarily so unlike ours, that some – though wrongly – high in the church say that it is only negatively, as being entirely different from everything else, that we can attach any meaning to the Name. This is not so; because the discoveries of science, their enabling us to *predict* what will be the course of nature, is proof conclusive that, though we cannot think any thought of God's, we can catch a fragment of His Thought, as it were.

Now such being the pragmaticist's answer to the question what he means by the word "God," the question whether there really *is* such a being is the question whether all physical science is merely the figment – the arbitrary figment – of the students of nature, and further whether the *one* lesson of the Gautama Boodha, Confucius, Socrates, and all who from any point of view have had their ways of conduct determined by meditation upon the psysico-psychical universe, be only their arbitrary notion or be the Truth behind the appearances which the frivolous man does not think of; and whether the super-human courage which such contemplation has conferred upon priests who go to pass their lives with lepers and refuse all offers of rescue is mere silly fanaticism, the passion of a baby, or whether it is strength derived from the power of the truth. Now the only guide to the answer to this question lies in the power of the passion of love which more or less overmasters every

[35] See below and 1.322.

agnostic scientist and everybody who seriously and deeply considers the universe. But whatever there may be of *argument* in all this is as nothing, the merest nothing, in comparison to its force as an appeal to one's own instinct, which is to argument what substance is to shadow, what bedrock is to the built foundations of a cathedral. (6.502-3.)

We have already examined briefly the opening thought concerning the pragmatic meaning of the word God. The point is well-taken, if in need of more examination. One would want to consider an analogous treatment of words which positivists would put in a similar category, words like: Satan, angel, soul, ghost, fairy. Do these words become meaningful too? If so , is there any word which can be discarded by the pragmatic criterion, or is it a tool for explication only?

But what can be said concerning the suggestion that, logically, to believe in science is to believe in God; or, as he puts it, that the man who rejects God must suppose science to be the "arbitrary figment" of the student of nature? Perhaps Peirce meant to suggest that if one accepts realism in principle, as the working scientist must, then realism will have theism as its final and reasonable conclusion, just as the man who accepts nominalism is impelled toward an ever deeper scepticism.

And the next point, the "power of the truth" which has led men to acts of greatness and self-sacrifice, and which leads the rest of us to admire and applaud them – it is hardly possible to name any school-book philosophy which has shown this power to anything like the same degree nor have any of those systems had any great effect for good upon men of all classes and conditions, even when they have affected for good some in the intelligentsia. Is this the power of "Truth" or of illusion? That illusion can be powerful, no one can deny, but *is it powerful for good* and is its power *constructive*? To affirm this in any strong sense is perhaps the final degree of scepticism – though of course the sceptic could only affirm it in a manner of speaking, since he knows not what is good or constructive. The whole point must be examined in the light of James' *Varieties of Religious Experience* – a book which opens the way to inquiry to a wonderful degree, and that not necessarily from James' remarks alone, but from the facts themselves which are presented.

Peirce acknowledges that his whole approach toward the question of God's existence depends upon the assumption that other minds will react to the hypothesis just as his does. He says that "... a latent tendency toward belief in God is a fundamental ingredient of the soul, and that, far from being a vicious or superstitious ingredient, it is simply the natural precipitate of meditation upon the origin of the Three Universes," and he adds that he believes this to be a fact characteristic of "universal human nature." (6.487) And again, he comments, "I have not pretended to have any other ground for my belief . . . than my assumption, which each one of us makes, that my own intellectual disposition is normal. I am forced to confess that no pessimist will agree with me. I do not admit that pessimists are, at the same time, thoroughly sane, and in addition are endowed in normal measure with intellectual vigor. . . ." (6.484)

Actually, the assumption that human minds are essentially similar is less a matter of "optimism" and "pessimism" than it is another case of realism versus the sceptical approach to the world, which is, I take it, what Peirce was really saying. To argue from analogy that human minds are probably about as similar as human hands can have no effect upon one who refuses to draw analogies or generalizations on principle. In the case of God's existence, if its popular acceptability as a theory is granted, the nominalist can always point to this as the best illustration of the phenomenon of the big lie. It all depends on how one looks at the world.

In summary, Peirce believed that the hypothesis of God arises in precisely the same way as any scientific hypothesis arises, only differing from the ordinary hypothesis in that its "Plausibility . . . reaches an almost unparalleled height among deliberately formed hypotheses." (6.489)

What, then, are some conceivable consequences that can be deduced from this idea? How is it connected with reality? Peirce openly admits that in *this* case the hypothesis is so vague that only in "exceptional cases" can one deduce a *definite* consequence. Conscious, no doubt, that this is not a very satisfactory answer, Peirce now plays his trump card, and this trump card is nothing but his wide formulation of the pragmatic maxim. The hypothesis of God, Peirce points out, has a

commanding influence over the whole conduct of life of its believers. According to that logical doctrine which the present writer first formulated in 1873 and named Pragmatism, the true meaning of any product of the intellect lies in whatever unitary determination it would impart to practical conduct under any and every conceivable circumstance, supposing such conduct to be guided by reflexion carried to an ultimate limit. (6.490)

Thus, *Peirce never abandoned his pragmatic maxim*, nor did he ever find it necessary to reword it or even reinterpret it: all he ever had to do was to draw attention to its specific wording. The meaning of a notion consists in all its *conceivable* consequences, in "any and every" conceivable consequence. These consequences are not limited to a laboratory, but extend to all human conduct as well, including, and especially including, mental conduct.

Needless to say, positivistically inclined commentators are sadly distressed by the way Peirce gets himself out of this bind. Manley Thompson says, "It is not easy to see how this circumstance [that the hypothesis has a "commanding influence over the whole conduct of life of its believers" (6.490)], if granted, can afford a scientific test of the hypothesis and counteract its being unverifiable in the ordinary sense." [36] But he later admits that there is some point to this way of viewing the matter.[37] And Buchler tries to make a rather sharp distinction between Peirce's formulation of the maxim where he uses words like 'sensible,' 'operation,' and 'verification,' and the places where he uses words like 'conduct,' 'self-control,' 'habit,' and 'purpose.' [38] The answer to this effort to find conflicting strains in Peirce is given by Peirce himself when he says that if one accepts a *wide* interpretation of the pragmatic maxim, "from this original form every truth that follows from any of the other forms [of the maxim] can be deduced, while some errors can be avoided into which other pragmatists have fallen." (5.415)

John J. Fitzgerald's study of Peirce constrains him to argue most thoroughly and persuasively for what we also have seen as the broad interpretation of Peirce's pragmatic maxim. Fitzgerald says the broad interpretation was Peirce's intention from the beginning, although Peirce only emphasizes it in later writings. ". . . in his later writings Peirce noted that there was not so much need for clarity of thought as there was for a recognition of thirdness." [39]

That it was always Peirce's intention in the maxim to point to the widest possible set of "conceivable consequences," is shown in case after case. Consider this statement:

I do not see why prayer may not be efficacious, or if not the prayer exactly, the state of mind of which the prayer is nothing more than the expression, namely the soul's consciousness of its relation to God, which is nothing more than precisely the pragmatistic meaning of the name of God; so that, in that sense, prayer is simply calling upon the name of the Lord. (6.516)

I believe that Peirce knew very well that he was saying when he formulated his maxim, and, taken altogether, there is very little to commend Thompson's analysis of the problem we have been considering:

[36] Manley Thompson, *The Pragmatic Philosophy of C. S. Peirce* (Chicago: The University of Chicago Press, 1953), p. 143. Are we quite *clear* on what the "ordinary sense" of verifiability is?

[37] *Ibid.*

[38] Buchler, *op. cit.*, p. 153.

[39] *Peirce's Theory of Signs as Foundation for Pragmatism* (The Hague: Mouton and Co., 1966), p. 176.

When Peirce's constant injunctions to test truth experimentally are taken in a literal sense, they of course preclude any attempt to give a true account of man's ultimate end except as that course of action which human nature is biologically and socially compelled to follow. Peirce himself wavered as to how literally he shoud take his own injunction. . . .

The pragmatic maxim itself is an excellent case in point. Literally, this maxim appears to render any proposition scientifically meaningless that implies no specific practical effects which would constitute its experimental verification. Peirce's suspicion that his maxim was stoic and nominalistic is in this respect justified, but he was also correct in pointing out that the realism he had advocated at the same time was inconsistent with this interpretation of the maxim.[40]

Peirce had carefully warned his readers that his maxim "allows any flight of imagination, provided this imagination ultimately alights upon a possible practical effect; and thus many hypotheses may seem at first glance to be excluded by the pragmatical maxim that are not really so excluded." (5.196) In the eyes of some critics, Peirce's religious views may have been "flights of imagination" on Peirce's part, but Peirce had made careful provision for these beliefs, and to say that they have only a "rather tenuous" connection with his system [41] is once again to permit oneself to lop off whole sections of Peirce's thought without sufficient justification. Wennerberg very accurately observes that much hinges on what one means when one speaks of *"possible"* practical effects.[42]

The point at issue here is, of course, that the situation in which someone with a given belief would be surprised must be *possible* in some sense of this word. Peirce has not explicitly declared what kind of possibility – logical, empirical, etc. – he has in mind in this context. And one can of course give different interpretations of the pragmatic maxim depending upon how one interprets the concept of possibility in this context.[43]

For myself, I cannot help but believe that Paul Weiss has correctly caught the spirit of Peirce when he observes that, though a good hypothesis ought to be readily refutable, ought not to contain unnecessary or redundant features and ought, in some sense, to be open to experimental verification, yet "it need not avoid the assumption of unobserved, unobservable, and even incredible elements for without them there would be no history and no subatomic physics." [44]

---

[40] Thompson, *op. cit.,* p. 261.
[41] Hartshorne and Weiss, *op. cit.,* 6.4.
[42] Wennerberg, *op. cit.,* p. 139.
[43] *Ibid.,* Almost everything is possible in a logical sense. Unfortunately, Wernerberg does not go on to examine the implications of this observation of his.
[44] Paul Weiss, "The Logic of the Creative Process," in Wiener and Young, *op. cit.,* p. 178. Compare on this point 1.120; 21511n.; 2.642.

And again, one can point to the passage where Peirce says that he does not mean by a "practical consequence" a difference, for example, in the way one might *answer* a metaphysical *question* or a question about history: "Pragmatism is completely volitalized if you admit that sort of practicality." (5.33) It cannot be a "species of practicality that consists in one's conduct about words and modes of expression." (*Ibid.*) But this would have to be compared to another passage, equally interesting and suggestive, where he says that our *thinking* about an hypothesis "really consists in making experiments upon it." (1.322) This latter is in accord with his insistence, explained above in the section on "Faculties," that no ideas are caught whole, but must be surveyed and examined in the brain – as when one thinks about the statement that the shortest distance between two points is a straight line. Very well, then; a mere difference in words is not a practical difference; but what about a real difference in conception discovered by the experiment of thinking on an idea – an idea unable to be tested in the real world? (Not that the mind is not part of the "real world.") The question of absolute *vs.* relative motion is a good case in point. Again, perhaps the key to all this is that only *conceivable* practical consequences and differences must be available. Also it is quite possible that we will have to admit that if one takes the pragmatic maxim in the wide sense which Peirce usually gives it, it seems to lose most of its value in determining the *admissibility* of hypotheses – though it undoubtedly has value there – but rather has its main value in its use as a tool to teach us the *real meaning* of concepts – its value lies in *clarifying* notions and making us see what is really involved, in rescuing us from the hypnotic effect of philosophical jargon and long chains of reasoning involving highly abstruse conceptions. It is a means of bringing us back to earth and making us talk sense and explain ourselves in terms that have "cash value," or at least a "conceivable" cash value! No one, certainly, can deny that Peirce repeatedly asserted that an hypothesis must have testable consequences in order to be fit to be entertained. Again, no one denies that it is immensely helpful to have *directly* testable consequénces. But the problem is very grave, because almost everything seems to have consequences of some kind that are very indirectly testable. How, for example, can one test this proposed moral truth: "All men should love their neighbors as themselves."? As an hypothesis, it pre-eminently fits Peirce's suggestion that an hypothesis be "idealistic" rather than "materialistic" – a suggestion prompted by his conviction that "idealistic" hypotheses will in fact be more rich in testable consequences. (5.599*f*.) But just how one would go about testing this hypothesis is hard to say. Compare it with all other proposed moral maxims – see if they can't be subsumed under it? This would be a form of "observation" as real as any other, for Peirce. It is very interesting, and relevant to our problem, this suggestion that the best hypotheses are the "idealistic" ones rather than the "materialistic" ones. Compare on this point the contempt Peirce expresses for "mystical" theories, "by which," he says, "I mean all those which have no possibility of being *mechanically explained*." (6.125, in an essay of 1878. My emph.)

Or again consider Peirce's own theory of synechism. This is a highly metaphysical idea involving the notion that ideas spread, that all things evolve and grow, including "laws" themselves, that all things are in a continuum, and the idea of the importance of the phenomenon of habit-taking, basic to protoplasm and all other things as well. Peirce says of this theory,

Such is our guess of the secret of the sphynx. To raise it from the rank of philosophical speculation to that of a scientific hypothesis, we must show that consequences can be deduced from it with more or less probability which can be compared with observation. We must show that there is some method of deducing the characters of the law which could result in this way by the action of habit-taking on purely fortuitous occurrences, and a method of ascertaining whether such characters belong to the actual laws of nature. (1.410)

But the discussion which follows, to no one's surprise, yields no suggestion of a test which one might in any sense call "mechanical" or indeed any kind of test at all. But this is true of almost all of Peirce's "metaphysical" discussions and is his usual way of proceeding. One *must* suppose that his idea of testing a metaphysical hypothesis was broad and generous indeed.

In any case, one can't hold Peirce to too strict (or perhaps one should say, too materialistic) an interpretation of his testability criterion – not, at least if one has any inclination to save Peirce from the most blatant kind of contradiction – for no one can deny that he seriously proposed metaphysical hypotheses which cannot be tested in the way one tests chemical theories. It is probably best to look upon this suggestion of Peirce's as "only a step" in his wider system and approach – as he himself said in a late essay – a point of view ultimately valid, perhaps always helpful, but not always easy to apply to abstruse theories. In this essay of 1902 Peirce bears out these points. He says of his pragmatic maxim, that,

The doctrine appears to assume that the end of man is action – a stoical axiom which, to the present writer at the age of sixty, does not recommend itself as forcibly as it did at thirty. If it be admitted, on the contrary, that action wants an end, and that that end must be something of a general description, then the *spirit of the maxim itself,* which is that we must look to the upshot of our concepts in order rightly to apprehend them, would direct us towards *something different from practical facts, namely, to general ideas, as the true interpreters of our thought.* Nevertheless, the maxim has approved itself to the writer, after many years of trial, as of great utility in leading to a relatively high grade of clearness of thought. He would venture to suggest that it should always be put into practice with conscientious thoroughness, but that, when that has been done, and not before, *a still higher grade of clearness of thought can be attained* by remembering that the only ultimate good which the practical facts to which it directs attention can subserve is to further the development of concrete reasonableness; so that the meaning of the concept does not lie in any individual reactions at all, but in the manner in which those reactions contribute to that development. (5.3, my emph.)

These remarks ought to be given conclusive weight both because they reflect *his own consistent application* of the maxim, and because they show his mature evaluation of it. And if these remarks are given conclusive weight, we cease looking for "practical facts" as the *final* and *ultimate* interpreters of our thought, and rather look to "general ideas." All the maxim is really trying to say, its real "spirit," as Peirce puts it, is merely that we look to the "upshot of our concepts in order to apprehend them . . . ." I cannot but believe that this not only was Peirce's definitive view of the matter, but also that it is in harmony with the spirit and literal wording of the maxim ("*conceivable* practical consequences"), and moreover it is his only salvation from the positivism he claimed to disavow and *certainly never practiced.* It is useful to point out that even Buchler admits that Peirce's intention in the pragmatic maxim ought to be judged from Peirce's own application of it. He says,

Undoubtedly, Peirce's own writings on matters metaphysical ought not to be judged in place of his programmatic pronouncements where the latter are not adequate enough for us to estimate the relations between pragmatism and metaphysics. But it is worthwhile venturing the opinion that a metaphysics consistent with pragmatism will not intentionally be filled with statements like "Active law is efficient reasonableness, or in other words is truly reasonable reasonableness. Reasonable reasonableness is Thirdness as Thirdness" (5.121).[45]

Moreover, I am confident that what I have just said is *amply* borne out by the following note appended to his essay "How to Make Our Ideas Clear," and written in 1906. After stating the maxim, and using various forms of the word 'conceive" several times, he adds this note:

[45] Buchler, *op. cit.,* pp. 152f.

This employment five times over of derivates of *concipere* must then have had a purpose. In point of fact it had two. One was to show that I was speaking of meaning in no other sense than that of *intellectual purport*. The other was to avoid all danger of being understood as attempting to explain a concept by percepts, images, schemata, or by anything but concepts. I did not, therefore, mean to say that acts, which are more strictly singular than anything, could constitute the purport, or adequate proper interpretation, of any symbol. I compared action to the finale of the symphony of thought, belief being a demicadence. Nobody conceives that the few bars at the end of a musical movement are the *purpose* of the movement. They may be called its upshot. But the figure obviously would not bear detailed application. I only mention it to show that the suspicion I myself expressed ... after a too hasty rereading of the forgotten magazine paper, that it expressed a stoic, that is, a nominalistic, materialistic, and utterly philistine state of thought, was quite mistaken. (5.402n.3)

Thus in the end he defends his maxim against even his own narrow interpretation of it, or misinterpretation, by calling attention to its specific wording, and *renouncing his own suspicion* that it tended *toward nominalism*. He explains most clearly the sense in which 'practical' is to be taken. Concepts are to be explained by concepts!

* * *

Very slowly and *very* reluctantly current epistemologists are being driven to the same sort of position which Peirce attained. It is becoming apparent that we must look to conceivable experiences for our understanding of the meaning or import of conceptions, but it is equally clear that there is no way to dismiss metaphysical or religious conceptions as meaningless on this criterion. Any criterion which cuts off such conceptions is going to cut off subatomic physics too, as Weiss says. In a famous passage as rigorous an empiricist as Willard V. O. Quine says that "in point of epistemological footing the physical objects and gods differ only in degree and not in kind." [46] And I am constrained to agree with Murphy when he says that the pragmatic principle

was thus, in origin, a part not only of a theory of science but of a metaphysical system which was designed to show that scientific method itself presupposed a radical metaphysical idealism carrying obvious and explicit theological implications. The apparent empiricism of the *Popular Science Month-*

---

[46] *From a Logical Point of View* (Cambridge: Harvard University Press, 1953), p. 44. And see N. Goodman *The Structure of Appearance* (Cambridge: Harvard University Press, 1951) pp. 59-60.

ly series is a mask: Peirce's goal was the rebuilding of the world view in terms which were theological and metaphysical in the extreme.[47]

And if it is true, as Murphy states, that the theories of science which Peirce elaborated in the 1870's "are based upon an idealistic metaphysic and a theory of cognition which are radically opposed to classical empiricism," [48] then it is equally true that current theories of science, if not based upon an idealistic metaphysic, are certainly being driven most reluctantly far beyond Humean empiricism.

F. PEIRCE AND JAMES

In the back of the critics' minds there is often the haunting fear that the mere admission of a metaphysical hypothesis, or the assertion that as a notion it may have practical effects, may bring Peirce dangerously close to the position of William James. But with Peirce and his maxim there is nothing said about the *truth* of an hypothesis. An hypothesis may be a genuine hypothesis with *some* reason for its support, and in a certain sense it may even work without it being true. Any hypothesis, no matter how well confirmed, may be false. It was James and not Peirce who said, you can say of an idea ". . . either that 'it is useful because it is true' or that 'it is true because it is useful.' Both these phrases mean exactly the same thing." [49] This is a most un-Peircean notion. As far as I know, there is only one place where Peirce even suggests such a view. In one place (1.538) he says that the only justification for a judgment is that "it subsequently turns out to be useful." But, as Feibleman observes, "usefulness, in Peirce's meaning . . . usually proves to mean some step which aids in the discovery of truth. Indeed it would not be misleading to regard pragmatism as nothing more than the method that complements the correspondence theory of truth." [50] Feibleman's last point is well taken. Peirce always insisted on

[47] "Kant's Children: The Cambridge Pragmatists" *Transactions of the Charles S. Peirce Society* IV, 1, Winter 1968, p. 13. Paul Weiss differs somewhat from Murphy believing rather that Peirce was more or less driven, "belatedly," to see the importance of theism. He laments that Peirce did not come earlier to these discoveries, though he thinks Peirce's discussions of these matters is "most perceptive" if "somewhat surprising." (*Op. cit.*, p. 139) Thomas Knight apparently sees a religious motive in Peirce from the beginning: "Peirce hoped, through the development of his scientific philosophy to prepare the way for the unity of religion and science." *Charles Peirce* (N.Y.: Washington Square Press, 1965), p. 176. My own feel for Peirce suggests to me that Peirce was all along a deeply religious man whose basic philosophical motivations included the glorification of God.

[48] *Ibid.*, p. 14.

[49] William James, *Pragmatism* (New York: The World Publishing Co., 1955), p. 135.

[50] James Feibleman, *The Introduction to Peirce's Philosophy* (N.Y.: Harper and Bros., 1946), p. 294.

the objectivity of truth: "That truth consists in a conformity of something *independent of his thinking it to be so,* or any man's opinion on that subject." (5.211) And he immediately adds that the pragmatic translation of this is that truth is the ultimate result of inquiry. Whatever one says about this, it is not James' doctrine that what works is true, nor does it justify the fear that an hypothesis, just because it is a legitimate one or even because it has a high degree of confirmation, must forthwith be taken as true. "Doing" was never the "Be-all and End-all" for Peirce's version of pragmatism.

Arthur O. Lovejoy, in an essay, "What Is the Pragmaticist Theory of Meaning?" betrays an almost total failure to understand Peirce, when he attributes to him this Jamesian position that thought exists solely for the sake of action. Peirce would, in fact, agree with Lovejoy's own criticism of this doctrine, when Lovejoy says,

It is, in short, no more evident – if one is to employ such expressions – that thought exists in man "for the sake of" action than that action exists for the sake of thought; and it is (I suggest) more probable that neither exists solely for the sake of the other. But the acceptance of the assumption by Peirce becomes somewhat intelligible if one recalls the intellectual climate of the 1870's. . . .[51]

On this point a compromise seems to be possible between James and Peirce. Instead of making the radical statement that what works is true, it would be better to say (what James did say, though the more radical statement is more often quoted) that whatever works is *so far* true. "Any idea on which we can ride, so to speak; any idea that will carry us prosperously from any one part of our experience to any other part, linking things satisfactorily, working securely, simplifying, saving labor; is *true for just so much, true in so far forth,* true instrumentally." [52] This is to say that a doctrine or theory that works has caught some of the spectrum of truth. Newtonian physics, for example, is false ultimately, but is true for a certain range of phenomena within a certain range of accuracy. It catches a good deal of truth in a few formulae. This surely is the reason it works within a certain range of reality. In any case it is apparent that James' statement cannot be thrown out as obvious nonsense, and that for this very good reason: If one believes that what is true works – and this is surely not so controversial – then it is certainly true that whatever works over the long run shares in the truth, approaches the truth to some minimal

[51] Arthur O. Lovejoy, "What is the Pragmaticist Theory of Meaning? The First Phase," in Wiener and Young, *op. cit.,* p. 19.

[52] William James, *Pragmatism,* p. 49. My emph.

extent, *or at least* has a fighting chance of being true. The history of the world does not support the theory that falsehood and error *work* for very long. Error, it is commonly believed, has within it the seeds of failure and destruction, though these effects may not be immediate. Whoever believes this must surely seriously consider the corollary: that whatever does not fail over a period of time partakes in the truth – and even error while it succeeds, has, in a manner of speaking, that much truth to it, or again, *at least* that whatever does not fail over a period of time has a fighting chance of being true.[53] Two apparently different theories, neither of which *ever* failed, would have to be taken as two different ways of saying the same thing.

In summary, Peirce conceived of his pragmatic maxim in a wide sense. He had no intention of dismissing as meaningless all of man's most interesting problems. The primary purpose of his maxim was to clear up abstract notions by looking to their "upshot." Secondarily, the maxim served to show the meaninglessness of an hypothesis with no conceivable consequences. The only real problem in connection with this latter doctrine is in trying to find an example of an hypothesis with no conceivable consequences.

G. PEIRCE AND KANT

A comparision of Kant and Peirce enables us to discern some interesting parallels. In a certain sense, Peirce's notion of abduction may be seen as taking the place of Kant's notions of "understanding" and "reason." The role of these two faculties in Kant's scheme was to synthesize or unify a manifold, and the difference between them was only a difference in the kind of manifold they worked on. We have seen that for Peirce too the essence of the abductive process is its unifying character.

For Kant the synthesis yielded by the understanding is called "knowledge" because the understanding is in contact with the data of sense, and, in effect, confers objectivity upon them. The ideas of reason (God, the world, the soul), on the other hand, do not yield knowledge of these concepts, but only the idea of them as postulates. This inferiority in status is caused by the fact that reason works only upon the manifold presented to it by the understanding, and is thus one step removed from the manifold of sense, and therefore cannot constitute reality in the way the understanding does. Still, the mind is drawn to the ideas of reason with a power bor-

---

[53] There is a splendid discussion of the relation between Peirce and James with regard to the pragmatic maxim in Buchler's book, *op. cit.,* pp. 166-174.

dering on compulsion, and is free to use the ideas as regulators of thought, provided it does not succumb to the "uncritical" and "dogmatic" temptation of regarding them as real and proved. This limitation of knowledge parallels the positivistic streak in Peirce, where he wishes to exclude abductions which have no conceivable practical consequences, i.e., which are out of touch with conceivable sensory experience. I am not claiming that this "positivistic streak" is fundamental to Peirce, or was his considered view, but I do not deny he flirted with it at times, and I do call attention to the rough way it parallels Kant's distinction between the claims derived from the understanding and from reason.

It is interesting to see how close Peirce's mature view – his wide interpretation of his pragmatic maxim – is to what Kant's view would have been if he could have seen his way clear to acknowledge that reason has as much right to be "constitutive" of the manifold of the understanding as the understanding has to be constitutive of the manifold of sense. Peirce says, "Kant's distinction of regulative and constitutive principles is unsound." (3.215) [54]

A clue to this hypothetical outcome could be derived from an examination of the chapter on the regulative employment of the ideas of pure reason – a chapter which in many ways is the heart of the *Critique of Pure Reason*:

Kant says plainly that reason has to do with the understanding just as the understanding has to do with the manifold of the object. The understanding applies the categories to the manifold of experience and thus yields a unity. In the same way, reason takes the concepts of understanding and "orders" them, and "gives them that unity which they can have only if they be employed in their widest possible application, that is, with a view to obtaining totality in the various series." [55] Reason "unifies the manifold of concepts by means of ideas, positing a certain collective unity as the goal of the activities of the understanding." [56]

Reason, having no immediate relation to an object, therefore has no constitutive employment. Transcendental ideas of pure reason when regarded as constitutive are "dialectical" and "pseudo-rational." What reason does have is a regulative employment, namely, "that of directing the understanding towards a certain goal upon which routes marked out by all its rules converge, as upon their point of intersection. This point is indeed a mere idea, a *focus imaginarius*, from which, since it lies quite

---

[54] See Rulon Wells, "Peirce as an American," in Bernstein, *op. cit.*, p. 35.
[55] Immanuel Kant, *Critique of Pure Reason,* (London: Macmillan and Co., Ltd., 1961), Norman Kemp Smith, Trans., p. 533.
[56] *Ibid.*

outside the bounds of possible experience, the concepts of the understanding do not in reality proceed; none the less it serves to give to these concepts the greatest [possible] unity combined with the greatest [possible] extension." [57] Reason tends to be deluded into thinking that these converging lines actually do converge into a real point, lying just outside the field of empirically possible knowledge. This is an illusion, says Kant, but it is a necessary one, for how else can the understanding extend its knowledge and application beyond the mere separate data it knows? Reason wishes to systematize and subsume under as few principles as possible the knowledge obtained for us by the understanding. In fact reason wishes to subsume everything under one principle. The principles of unity "are not derived from nature; on the contrary, we interrogate nature in accordance with these ideas, and consider our knowledge as defective so long as it is not adequate to them." [58] In fact, Kant says, "the influence of reason on the classifications of the natural scientist is still easily detected." [59]

Reason is used apodeictically when it searches for particular cases of what it already certainly knows as a universal. One has only to judge whether the particular is a case of the generalization. On the other hand, reason is employed hypothetically when it knows certain particular cases with certainty, but the universal of these cases is problematic, a "mere idea." If all particular cases point to the universal rule, we are inclined to argue for it. This hypothetical use of reason is not constitutive – that is, it does not strictly *prove* the rule. "The hypothetical employment of reason is regulative only; its sole aim is, so far as may be possible, to bring unity into the body of our detailed knowledge, and thereby to *approximate* the rule to universality." [60] Kant says further that this systematic unity "is the *criterion of the truth of its rules*." [61] This unity is not given, but only "projected," and it aids us in the special modes of employment of the understanding, and directs "its attention to cases which are not given, and thus rendering it more coherent." [62]

Reason not only wishes to put detailed phenomena under various principles, but also wishes to put the principles all under one principle. But from all of this nothing can be inferred about the world: one is not

[57] *Ibid.* Compare all of this with abduction!
[58] *Ibid.*, p. 534. Here is Kant's subjectivism and nominalism, so much denounced by Peirce.
[59] *Ibid.*
[60] *Ibid.*, p. 535.
[61] *Ibid.* Compare Peirce: ". . . the validity of a conception consists in the impossibility of reducing the content of consciousness to unity without the introduction of it." (1.545).
[62] *Ibid.*

even permitted to "in a certain measure postulate this unity *a priori*." [63]

The way this doctrine works can be seen clearly in Kant's treatment of the self and of God. Here are two unities which bring under one idea a great diversity of phenomena. One does not say that these unities are necessarily to be met with, but merely that we must seek them "in the interest of reason." [64]

All of this takes on a new significance from a Peircean standpoint. Peirce has no use for the distinction between reason and understanding. He suggests that the hypotheses of perception are no different from the hypotheses of conception, that hypotheses of physics and hypotheses of metaphysics are of the same general kind and are to be judged by the same standards and treated in the same way. (See 3.215) In short, we are invited back into the realm of "dogmatism" – but with a difference: instead of making physics and metaphysics alike "dogmatic," Peirce treats them both as realms in which all our thinking is strictly hypothetical, and hence always fallible. Kant's work, of course, was all done in the service of finding indubitable foundations for knowledge, and he would never have been satisfied with less. More on this in the next chapter.

H. PEIRCE AND JOHN WISDOM

I have never seen John Wisdom refer to Peirce, but it is plain from his work that he has come to an epistemological position in some respects remarkably close to Peirce's. Particularly is it remarkable if he has done so independently. Wisdom's continual stress on the importance of interpretation, alias abduction, is found most dramatically in his two famous essays, "Gods," [65] and "The Logic of God." [66] In these essays he is at pains to stress that the question of God's existence is a perfectly legitimate question even if it doesn't lend itself to scientific test. It is a question not so much of what the data are but of how they are to be interpreted. How one decides the question depends on the light in which one views the world, and one's decision then itself becomes a controlling factor in how one sees things.

Here, to use an example of Wisdom's, is a man whose behavior is exemplary, with just those few lapses to be expected in any normal person. The suggestion is made that the man is a very talented spy. Some people

---

[63] *Ibid.*, p. 536. How one would do this sort of thing by "measures" is a hard question.

[64] *Ibid.*, p. 537.

[65] John Wisdom, *Philosophy and Psychoanalysis* (Berkeley: University of California Press, 1969), pp. 149-168.

[66] John Wisdom, *Paradox and Discovery* (Berkeley: University of California Press, 1970), pp. 1-23.

believe the suggestion, others don't. Those who trust the man point to his sincerity and earnestness in the cause, his genuine friendliness toward his companions. The others say, "Yes, we have heard that he has a real talent for feigning sincerity." Of course a case like this may be subject to conclusive proof eventually but in the meantime we may be forced into painful decisions as to whether to entrust this man with important missions, and we will have to make our decision on the basis of an interpretation of his behavior. In Peirce's terms, we will have to be guided by instinctively formed hypotheses.

I will not elaborate on Wisdom's example of the "invisible gardner," [67] for there is already a considerable literature grown up around this most stimulating example. But anyone who examines the example will see its bearing on Peirce's epistemology.

Wisdom raises the question, "When all the facts are known, can there still be a question of fact? [68] He answers, yes, there can still be the problem of how the facts are interpreted. We may know all the facts of how a person has behaved thus far, and still not know what his intention in this behavior is. We may know all the facts involved in an accident and still not know whether there was criminal neglect. We may know all the facts of science and still want to know whether there is some living intelligence behind all those facts.

Talk about religion and metaphysics may not directly alter our behavior but may drastically alter the way we perceive the world. A lady tries on a hat. She is confused whether she likes it or not. Her friend says, "My dear, it's the Taj Mahal!" Now she sees what's wrong. She knows the hat won't do – it's too elaborate, too fantastic, too something very hard to put into words or even to see unless some perceptive friend is around to jolt one's perception into focus.[69]

In a brilliant phrase Wisdom summarizes the case neatly when he says, "There is a logic of interpretation." As we live and breathe, this is abduction. Wisdom is at pains to show that he does not mean deduction or induction. It is plainly not enumeration, nor is it a deductive chain of argument, but it is like the legs of a chair supporting the chair mutually.[70]

As he says in the introduction to his book, *Paradox and Discovery*,

It is submitted that questions which "have no answers" may yet present problems which have solutions, that questions which "have no answers" can and, mostly, do evince some inadequacy in our apprehension of things, and

[67] "*Gods,*" pp. 154ff.
[68] "*Gods,*" pp. 156f.
[69] "*Logic,*" pp. 2ff.
[70] "*Gods,*" p. 157.

that when this inadequacy is removed by thought, which while it is helped by precedent is not bound by it, we gain a new view of what is possible and sometimes of what is actual.[71]

This is very well said. Wisdom is a subtle and marvelously provocative writer. His work deserves a thorough study and commentary by someone, but this is not the occasion for it. But readers are most earnestly directed to his work for further elaboration of the sorts of themes we are developing in this book. Wisdom is destined to be recognized as a truly original and incisive philosopher, and no time spent on his work will be lost.

[71] p. ix.

CHAPTER III

FALLIBILISM:
THE SELF-CORRECTIVE FEATURE OF THOUGHT

A. THE NOTION OF "MEANING" EXAMINED ON PEIRCEAN PRINCIPLES

We have already achieved a preliminary understanding of Peirce's treatment of "meaning," but since this topic has been a major preoccupation of twentieth century philosophy we will go into the matter in more detail. In what follows we offer a very brief outline of major schools of thought on the subject. What they all have in common is a tendency to equate "meaning" with "usage" in different senses of this latter term. It is interesting to see this problem from a Peircean viewpoint, and the suggested answer to the problem which we present below is obviously based upon Peirce's analysis of such related concepts as "rule," "idea," "*conceivable* practical consequences," etc. But rather than anticipating our conclusion here, let us rather lead up to it.

1. *Meaning and usage*

Nominalism is a doctrine presupposed by much English-speaking philosophy. Since nominalism admits only the existence of particulars, we find ourselves at once in an awkward position when we come to examine concepts such as those of meaning or law. For it is hard to see how the meaning of a word or a law of nature can be a particular thing or event. It is no doubt possible to approach a philosophical difficulty such as this from the standpoint of a radical empiricism with its consequent nominalism, and on this program to say and discover many interesting things. But, as Hume's example very well shows us, progress in the untanglement of philosophical difficulties is well-nigh impossible with those presuppositions.

But let us start from the beginning and inquire just what constitutes the meaning of a word or other symbol. Common sense suggests that the meaning of a word [1] is a certain given "concept" or "idea" which one may "have in mind." Almost every philosopher of reputation, however, has pointed out the ambiguity of the word "concept" and the misleadingness of the phrase "in the mind" ("as in a box?" etc.). Of course, the meaning of a word is a concept, an idea. Words stand for and express ideas. This is elementary.

Again, the controversy over "meaning" is not to be answered by saying that the meaning of a word is a certain set of other words which by convention are taken as equivalent to the word in question. In one sense that would be the meaning of a word, but then what would be the meaning of this definition?

If, then, in order to avoid the circularity of mere words, we say that the meaning of a word is a certain concept or idea, we then have the question of what "concepts" or "ideas," themselves are. What is the nature of an idea?

We are all aware that a consensus has developed in the past fifty years to the effect that the meaning of a concept consists, not in another set of words, nor in a mental image (which simply isn't there in most cases), but rather, in the *use* of the concept. The "meaning" of a concept is its use.

In a rough way we accept this suggestion, and we wish in the following remarks to elaborate upon some of the different ways this suggestion has been and can be understood. Among these various ways, some are much to be preferred to others.

As we have seen, the pragmatists, now outcast, were the first to make the suggestion. The "cash value" of a word or concept was for them the difference it made in life and action. No difference in life, no difference in meaning. James' version of this doctrine was and is too vague and too subject to criticism to stand the test of time, but the key idea remains. The positivists, however, have taken the suggestion and applied a certain rigor to its analysis. For the positivists, the meaning of an idea was, alternatively, (1) its method of direct verification, or (2) its method of indirect verification, or (3) its method of falsification. Unfortunately, the rigor of the positivists succeeded only in showing that false notions cannot be verified, and true ones cannot be falsified. This yields the curious consequence that

[1] In the following discussion we overlook a world of subtle difficulties connected with relational words and words which function only in the context of a sentence. It is only in an extended sense that we may speak of many of these words, taken alone and apart from their function in the language, as "having meaning." The following discussion is largely concerned with paradigm cases of simple nouns, adjectives, and verbs – but what is true of these is true of all words to a degree and in a sense.

either true or false statements are meaningless, depending on whether one goes the verification route or the falsification route.

However, the rigor of the positivists has not been in vain. For the painstaking effort to implement the positivist program – that is, to achieve some formulation of the positivist maxim consonant with the spirit of the movement, with the practice of science and also, if possible, with the usages and understandings of common sense, minimally qualified, – the effort, I say, to implement this impossible program has failed for one illuminating reason: *the generality intrinsic to words and concepts could not be caught in any maxim based upon empiricistic principles narrowly understood.* Positivism could not and cannot find a place for *disposition* statements, or statements of *law*. Moreover, any attempt to translate scientific notions into purely operational terms runs square into this same difficulty, namely, that a scientific notion may, and usually does, in the interesting cases, entail a potentially infinite variety of possible operations.

Those and related difficulties lay behind Wittgenstein's abandonment of positivism. Also, he had seen that words and concepts are intrinsically *vague,* their meaning altering in subtle ways with their context, and their meaning in no wise to be caught either in tight verbal definition or a tight operational or experimental definition, unless this was done arbitrarily and by *fiat.* That is, one could decree that a word should mean such and such (and this procedure is sometimes useful and necessary), but such artifical meanings could not be counted as the complete meaning of the concept in real life.[2] The meaning of a word thus came to be understood by Wittgenstein and his disciples as the word's very use in the language. The meaning was not a thing, or an image, or another set of words, or a set of (scientific) consequences but was rather the very ways the word functioned in language.

Although this doctrine has been very influential, it has yet seemed to many a somewhat strange affair. Surely the very *significance* of a word, its import, the idea which lay behind it, cannot be said to be merely the manner it functions in the language. Common sense can not but suppose that language is the mere external expression and symbolism of *something in the mind,* whether we call this something concepts, meanings, or whatever. We may repeat here again that it a mere truism to say that words stand for ideas, or, in other words have meanings. The crucial question here really is what is the nature of a meaning.

The three theories we have outlined here have a good deal in common.

---

[2] Cf. John Wisdom's point that the search for the meaning of a concept is sometimes very like the search for a *policy* or for a ruling by a judge. A *decision* is called for, but it need not be arbitrary. See "Gods," pp. 157f.

They all look away from mental images or mental entities of any sort, and look rather, as good empiricists should, toward outward, public occurrences. One is tempted here to say, "toward outward, public occurrences *manifesting* the meaning or idea," but it is the point of each of these doctrines to leave off references to these alleged internal entities ("meanings") and say what needs to be said only in terms of public phenomena. Some advocates of these views are reductionists who go far as to say that the ideas are *nothing but* their outward manifestations; others say only that outward manifestations are all we can know about "ideas" and all we should, as empirical philosophers, be concerned with.

If we permit ourselves a rough generalization, we may also say that these three views also agree in characterizing meanings or concepts by their *use*. Each of these three parties has a somewhat different understanding of the notion "use" – the pragmatists thinking of use in everyday life, the positivists thinking of the rigorously controlled usages and operations of science, and the analysts thinking primarily of the use of the word in common language. But the kinship of these views is worthy of note.

There can hardly be any doubt that the exhaustive analysis which these three parties have bestowed upon this key concept has illuminated our understanding of the point in question. What these analyses have tried to accomplish, in particular, is to show us that the meaning of a word is not just some static, abstract essence entertained by the contemplative eye of the mind. Perhaps, indeed, they have not shown that ideas are *not* such creatures, but they have looked to outward results for empirically respectable translations or manifestations of such creatures, which anyway can then be banished – *for all they are are their manifestations.*

Let us consider how these views depart from common sense. In the first place, it seems that one could learn how to use a word in the language and still never truly understand the notion for which it stood. Perhaps such is the case with the congenitally blind who speak of the colors. At least we can say that their understanding of a word such as "red" is in some sense seriously deficient even if they use the word correctly. Moreover, it seems too that we have a very satisfactory intuitive understanding of many notions which the positivists have not succeeded in translating into operational terms – witness the positivist's retreat from "hard" versions of the maxim to "soft" versions, and for that matter the disintegration of the movement in its robust forms. To summarize the common sense feeling on this matter in a few words, we may say that when the mind grasps a meaning something inward seems to happen which cannot be translated adequately into any mere manifestations or series of manifestations. One knows when one has passed from not understanding to understanding. When a meaning is grasped, when something is understood, one knows that one is now capable of using the notion correctly, not only in language and life, but also in thought. But what is it exactly that has happened when one has passed from incomprehension to comprehension?

2. Meaning as Law[3]

To answer this question briefly, albeit in a very unEnglish fashion, we urge that a *law, habit,* or *principle* has been established in the mind. Now just as the law of gravity cannot really and adequately be characterized as a simple series of manifestations, but must rather be considered as a permanent possibility of manifestations, i.e., a law or tendency, so also an understanding or a meaning cannot be characterized adequately by any finite series of its manifestations but represents, or rather *is*, a *rule* of action or thought, with a potential applicability to an infinitude of different conditions.

The notion that the meaning of a concept consists in its *use,* in whatever of the above three prominent interpretations one gives to that word, certainly represents a significant philosophical advance – an advance, moreover, which has been made in the face of the empiricist's general unwillingness to allow the existence of anything except particulars. But analysis has shown beyond doubt that the meaning of a word is not a particular, neither a particular mental image, nor a particular verbal definition nor any one particular operation.

Nor can we really say that the meaning of a concept is nothing but its uses *serially connected together.* Rather, we must ask, "Is there any *principle* or *law* regulating and underlying these many uses of a concept?" Here, as we have seen, radical empiricists face a severe embarrassment, for they must analyze laws into their manifestations, *serially* and, in the last analysis, *arbitrarily connected together,* with a highly troublesome "and so on" attached to the end of the given series.

No, we must admit that there is something in the mind corresponding to our words and concepts, and this "something" is no particular object or image, but is more like a habit or tendency (to use words ordinarily applied to persons), or, more accurately, a law, rule, or principle. When

[3] William Paul Haas, O.P., has a quite good study of Peirce centering around Peirce's conception of law. This is a fundamental theme in Peirce and eminently worth the student's attention inasmuch as English philosophy of science has been utterly deficient on this point. Haas's book is *The Conception of Law and the Unity of Peirce's Philosophy* (South Bend, Ind.: The University of Notre Dame, 1964).

the meaning of a concept "dawns" on a person, when he "catches on" to an idea, a kind of regulative principle has been established in the mind, – regulative, that is, of his future talk, conduct, and thought on that particular subject.

We may imagine a learned man who has spent fifty years in research on the honeybee. Now suppose a very ignorant citydweller asks this learned man what a honeybee is. Now, bad theories of meaning arose in the past precisely because the temptation is strong to suppose that the meaning of the term "honeybee" is primarily the *image* we may form in our minds of this insect. And indeed the insect's shape, size and coloring are among the most prominent features of our concept if it. But of course even the layman's concept of the insect is much richer than that, including particularly such things as that bees sting, live in hives, feed on nectar, produce honey, etc. (And that "*etc.*" has some real importance, as we have seen)! And the specialist's concept of the honeybee is richer still. Indeed, insofar as his knowledge is accurate, the plan, characteristics, features, qualities of the honeybee are reproduced in his mind – not indeed as mere mental images, but as laws of conduct – conduct of the bee, but the laws expressing themselves in conduct of the scientist, including the conduct of his thought. In a real sense the same laws that are "in" the bee or that constitute the bee are also in the scientist's mind. Laws of course are timeless and placeless and may be two or more places at once.

We may remember at this point Berkeley's wonderful argument to the effect that we have no concept of a triangle! Any triangle we imagine, says he, will be either scalene, isosoles, or obtuse, whereas we mean by triangle any of these but none in particular. Hence the argument that "triangle" is only a name, a word. In fact, of course, we do have a concept of a triangle (any three-sided plane figure) although we can't translate this concept into an image in the mind. The word "any" makes that impossible. But the concept can be grasped, understood, comprehended. This understanding is a kind of rule of conduct, guiding our talk, our actions, and our thinking about triangles. We might think of it as a rule for constructing and manipulating triangles. This rule is not, as a Humean might urge, just all of our triangle conduct added together, but exists in its own right as a rule, – somehow. It exists in the same way that habits or dispositions exist in people, even when not being actualized.

It is a very interesting thing to see empiricists wrestle themselves free from nominalism to the point where they will say that the meaning of a term is its *usage*. But like Hume who spoke so freely of habit and custom, they see not that usage, habit and custom are non-particulars, universals, and that acknowledging their existence in one's ontology opens the door to the *literal reality* of laws, relations, species, and heaven knows what other non-empirical creatures – creatures which can be grasped only with the mind's eye, and never with the senses.

B. ORGANISM AND INTERDEPENDENCE IN KNOWLEDGE

Peirce is a strange amalgam of the English temperament with the Continental temperament, but the English is predominant. One can see how easy it would have been for Peirce to become another Kant, especially in style, but also to a degree in substance. Indeed there are traces of this everywhere in Peirce's work, especially in those passages where he lapses into deep obscurity and begins to make up new and terrible expressions at a furious rate, where his sense of humor fails and his humanity disappears. Nor are these always his best passages. But they are the exceptions. The bulk of Peirce's work is English in spirit – lively, witty, clear, insouciant, impudent, full of love of style and hatred of nonsense.

This is not a mere matter of literary style, but it is true of philosophical style. It would be difficult if not impossible to imagine Hume reading Kant's philosophy with profit. Needless to say, Hume would not have liked the man – so dry, humorless, pedantic, arrogant, expounding a system so incredible in a style so barbaric. On the other hand, whether Hume could have read Peirce with profit is purely a matter of conjecture, but at least it is not impossible to imagine. As seen from the viewpoint of one who genuinely enjoys the temperament and style of both men it is hard not to believe that they would have liked and respected one another, and it does not seem to one with this viewpoint that Hume could have dismissed Peirce's line of argument with contempt, but rather might very well have been impressed by it. Pure conjecture, indeed, but possible; and possibly true not only for Hume, but also for the other Englishmen – Berkeley, Locke, Reid, Mill, Bentham. But can one believe it of Hegel?! It is not possible.

Peirce's deep interest in and respect for science and logic immediately put him upon the English side of the philosophical fence.

I am saturated, through and through, with the spirit of the physical sciences. I have been a great student of logic, having read everything of any importance on the subject, devoting a great deal of time to medieval thought, without neglecting the works of the Greeks, the English, the Germans, the French, etc., and have produced systems of my own both in deductive and inductive logic. (1.3)

Peirce's hard-headedness, his dislike of mysticism, his tendency to treat small issues and to support a large generalization upon many small considerations rather than upon one grand logical step – all of these things make him English. At bottom it is a matter of style and approach more than anything else that makes him English, especially since, in his conclusions, he almost never agrees with them, except for Reid, and here only to a degree. But he does not agree with the Continentals in conclusions either – he is closer to the medievals perhaps than any modern group, especially on the overriding issue of realism *vs.* nominalism. He is an empiricist more than a rationalist, but he abhors the common-law marriage of empiricism and nominalism. Nominalists have always tended toward empiricism, but from Peirce's point of view the marriage is tragically sterile, for, although the nominalists go to experience, they have made up their minds beforehand to learn nothing from it. At one point Peirce deplores "the superficial perspicuity of [nominalistic] metaphysics [which] rendered [Mill's] logic extremely popular with those who think, but do not think profoundly; who know something of science, but more from the outside than the inside, and who for one reason or another delight in the simplest theories even if they fail to cover the facts." (1.70)

Again, after relating how diligently he had studied Kant, he says,

The effect of these studies was that I came to hold the classical German philosophy to be, upon its argumentative side, of little weight; although I esteem it, perhaps am too partial to it, as a rich mine of philosophical suggestions. The English philosophy, meagre and crude, as it is, in its conceptions, proceeds by surer methods and more accurate logic. The doctrine of the association of ideas is, to my thinking, the finest piece of philosophical work of the pre-scientific ages. Yet I can but pronounce English sensationalism to be entirely destitute of any solid bottom. (1.5)

But perhaps the passage which best expresses Peirce's ambivalent feelings toward the sceptical, "tough-minded" thinkers is the following:

There is a strong tendency in us all to be sceptical about there being any real meaning or law in things. This scepticism is strongest in the most masculine thinkers. I applaud scepticism with all my heart, provided it have four qualities: first, that it be sincere and real doubt; second, that it be aggressive; third, that it push inquiry; and fourth, that it stand ready to acknowledge what it now doubts, as soon as the doubted element comes clearly to light. To be angry with sceptics, who, whether they are aware of it or not, are the best friends of spiritual truth, is a manifest sign that the angry person is himself infected with scepticism – not, however, of the innocent and wholesome kind that tries to bring truth to light, but of the mendacious, clandestine, disguised, and conservative variety that is afraid of truth, although truth merely means the way to attain one's purposes. If the sceptics think that any account can be given of the phenomena of the universe while they leave Meaning out of account, by all means let them go ahead and try to do it. It is a most laudable and wholesome enterprise. But when they go so far as to say that there is no such idea in our minds, irreducible to anything else, I say to them, "Gentlemen, your strongest sentiment, to which I subscribe with all my heart, is that a man worthy of that name will not allow petty intellectual predilections to blind him to truth, which consists in the conformity of his thought to his purposes. But you know there is such a thing as a defect of candor of which one is not oneself aware. You perceive, no doubt, that if there be an element of thought irreducible to any other, it would be hard, on your principles, to account for man's having it, unless he derived it from environing Nature. But if, because of that, you were to turn your gaze away from an idea that shines out clearly in your mind, you would be violating your principles in a very much more radical way." (1.344)

There is a sense, indeed, in which the English have been pre-eminently the "most masculine" thinkers, the tough-minded philosophers, but there is another sense in which most of philosophy in the 17th-19th centuries has been tough-minded. The English have got this reputation by the fact that so often they come to conclusions which seem to have so little in them to comfort man – whatever comfort they give is mostly of the kind that comes from knowing the worst. But the sense in which most of the classical philosophers deserve this title is in this regard: that they long for *certain* conclusions, for an unshakable foundation on which to build a worldview. This of course is a natural desire – man has always hated doubt and uncertainty – but it was a natural desire made more intense by the development of science and mathematics with their apparent success in winning a consensus and, their being, if not at present in full possession of all the truth, at least on the right track toward the truth with every reason to hope for eventual success. This was much more than could be said about philosophy, and every philosopher looked upon himself as the very man to put an end to the scandal by setting metaphysics in order once and for all.

But it was this passionate desire to follow the *mathematical model*, to have a system with indubitable foundations and a logically air-tight development – it was this misguided effort which lead to the most pernicious results. Chief among these results was the recurring tendency toward solipsism, subjectivity, and scepticism. Most of these philosophers thought of themselves as being "scientific" men, and in their minds the methods of the physical scientist and the mathematician were vaguely conceived to be similar (as indeed they are in a vague way). But from the hindsight

Peirce affords, it is clear that a basic misunderstanding of methods was involved here. The process of deduction is infallible in principle (*only* in principle), but is applicable mainly in the (apparently) self-contained world of the mathematician and logician. But the process of induction, and even more particularly of abduction, is, by its very nature, fallible.

1. *Self-correction*

Among the most brilliant and provocative of all of Peirce's essays is the one he called, "The First Rule of Logic." (5.574*ff*.) This essay touches issues the most elemental. In it Peirce attempts to explicate the nature of inductive reasoning, and in the process he tries, as so many men have done before him, to lay the ax to the root of scepticism. Any original effort in this direction can only be of great interest to serious thinkers.

The main point of this profound essay can be put so simply that it sounds like a cliché or worse, and in fact it is a point that is in perfect accord with common sense – which is to say it is not in accord with much of what has passed for philosophy. But like all basic truths, if indeed it be a truth, it has enormous implications, particularly in that almost all of modern philosophy has been accomplished upon the opposite assumption, implicitly if not explicitly.

That main point is this: *the more one reasons, the nearer to the truth one is likely to come.* How indeed can this apparent platitude have a claim to greatness? Because sceptical philosophers and philosophers who pattern their work after the mathematical model, which, to a large degree, includes any number of modern systems, do so at the expense of ignoring many of their most fundamental themes which, if taken seriously, would preclude the use of that assumption.

Hume, more clearly than anyone, denied the maxim. In his masterpiece, *A Treatise of Human Nature*,[4] he argues essentially that all knowledge is merely probable. But then the knowing process by which we judge that a thing is probable is itself a process subject to error. Thus the judgment that a thing is probable is itself merely probable. Then one may pass judgment upon the cumulative weight of these two probabilities, and even then judge that the whole complex is still very highly probable. But what about this last judgment of the complex of judgments? It too is merely probable, but less probable than the preceeding judgments. Thus one is led into an infinite regress "till at last there remain nothing of the

---

[4] David Hume, *A Treatise of Human Nature*, L. A. Selby-Bigge, ed., (Oxford: At the Clarendon Press, 1888), pp. 180ff.

original probability, however great we may suppose it to have been, and however small the diminution by every new uncertainty." [5] As Peirce puts it:

You might as well say at once that reasoning is to be avoided because it has led to so much error; quite in the same philistine line of thought would that be; and so well in accord with the spirit of nominalism that I wonder some one does not put it forward. (1.383)

Hume's view of this matter is hidden in many ancient and respectable philosophers. Aquinas says, "A small mistake in the beginning is a great one in the end, according to the Philosopher in the first book of the *De Caelo et Mundo.*" [6] It is a small step from believing this to believing that one ought not reason at all. In fact, to understand in a word the point Peirce makes in this essay one has merely to deny this sentiment of Aquinas and Aristotle. Bertrand Russell puts the same point in a whimsical way, but though he means to be whimsical (I assume), he has stated Hume's literal view, and one can only wonder if Russell knows what he is saying – that is, does he really have a bone fide reply to this argument:

Logic was, formerly, the art of drawing inferences; it has now become the art of abstaining from inferences, since it has appeared that the inferences we naturally feel inclined to make are hardly ever valid. I conclude, therefore, that logic ought to be taught in schools with a view to teaching people not to reason. For, if they reason, they will almost certainly reason wrongly.[7]

This way of looking at the matter is fostered by the model of mathematics and geometry, and it is an approach that has pervaded philosophy since the times of Euclid himself, if not before. In any kind of deductive scheme, error in the premises can only lead to more and more errors, and any error introduced into the chain of reasoning will likewise ruin the conclusion or conclusions, and the ruin will become more disastrous the further the chain of reasoning is carried.

Clearly, on the other hand, ordinary scientific reasoning is a self-corrective process. The more one learns, the more one corrects one's presuppositions. For Peirce this is not only true of scientific methodology, but true also of thinking in general. All thinking is self-corrective. If true, this would be a wonderful discovery, showing at once the futility of the scep-

[5] *Ibid.*, p. 182.
[6] Thomas Aquinas, *On Being and Essence,* Armand Maurer, trans., (Toronto: the Pontifical Institute of Medieval Studies, 1949), p. 25.
[7] Bertrand Russell, *Sceptical Essays* (London: George Allen and Unwin, Ltd., 1938), pp. 66f.

tical method in philosophy as well as the futility of the ratio-deductive
method, and confirming the inductive, so-called "scientific" method.

But how can we say that *all* thought partakes of this self-corrective
feature, particularly when deduction seems not to be self-corrective at all,
but seems rather to lead one further and further away from the truth with
the introduction of even one error into the chain of reasoning? In answering this, Peirce gives a diagramatically simple case. Imagine a column of
figures to be added. No one adding them together, unless he is very accustomed to doing sums, will be absolutely sure that the result is accurate,
and, if accuracy is very important, he will want to add it up a couple of
times or use one of the systems designed to check addition. But what in
the world is this but taking a vote, a sample? It is actually a form of induction. The same thing applies to any deductive chain. In a geometrical
proof one equally feels the compulsion to go back and check the reasoning.
To be sure, a deduction is *theoretically* infallible, but this is never anything
more than a *theoretical infallibility*. In practice, error may creep into
even the most simple deduction -- in fact errors are every so often found
in mathematical proofs of the most rigorous kind which had been thought
accurate for generations. (*Cf.* 1.248)

Is it possible, then, that two plus two does not equal four? Certainly it
is *possible,* says Peirce. (2.197) It is possible that two plus two is not equal
to four, but we do not doubt it for a moment. Mathematical reasoning is
beyond all doubt, but fallible. (*Cf.* 7.108*f.*; 2.192) Similarly, we may be
quite confident that most of our common sense beliefs are true, but we
cannot be sure which ones. (4.63; 5.311)

This whole line of reasoning is strongly reinforced by all of the arguments Peirce used in the "Faculties" essay to show that all reasoning of
whatever kind must be fallible because of the fact that thinking is a
process in time.

But what of Peirce's contention that the ratiocinative process, the more
it is pursued, tends not only to correct its conclusions, but also *even the
premises from which it starts?* On this point Peirce observes:

The theory of Aristotle is that a necessary conclusion is just equally as certain
as its premises, while a probable conclusion is somewhat less so. Hence, he
was driven to his strange distinction between what is better known to Nature
and what is better known to us. But were every probable inference less
certain than its premises, science, which piles inference upon inference, often
quite deeply, would soon be in a bad way. Every astronomer, however, is
familiar with the fact that the catalogue place of a fundamental star, which
is the result of elaborate reasoning, is far more accurate than any of the
observations from which it was deduced. (5.575)

And of even more moment is Peirce's assertion that not only can reason correct the premises from which it starts, but reason can also perfect its own techniques! (2.195)

Peirce gives an example of even a mathematical process into which random errors may be introduced, but which tends to correct itself the longer it is pursued. But he admits that the process of correcting premises is not, "so sure, or at least so swift," in a deductive chain as in an inductive argument. But he still maintains that even deduction is self-corrective:

Deductive inquiry, then, has its errors; and it corrects them too. But it is by no means so sure, or at least so swift to do this as in Inductive science. A celebrated error in the *Mechanique Celeste* concerning the amount of theoretical acceleration of the moon's mean motion deceived the whole world of astronomy for more than half a century. Errors of reasoning in the first book of Euclid's Elements, the logic of which book was for two thousand years subjected to more careful criticism than any other piece of reasoning without exception ever was or probably ever will be, only became known after the non-Euclidean geometry had been developed. *The certainty of mathematical reasoning, however, lies in this, that once an error is suspected, the whole world is speedily in accord about it.* (5.577, my emph.)

Peirce does not mean that there is a "logical" possibility for error in deductive reasoning; only that the one doing the reasoning, whether man or machine, may introduce an error. But however the error may get there, it is still an error at the end and the whole process is fallible. A chain is as weak as its weakest link. There is a temptation to say that there is something very Hegelian about Peirce's view of the process of coming to the truth. Peirce says,

This calls to mind one of the most wonderful features of reasoning and one of the most important philosophemes in the doctrine of science, of which, however, you will search in vain for any mention in any book I can think of; namely, that reasoning tends to correct itself, and the more so, the more wisely its plan is laid. Nay, it not only corrects its conclusions, it even corrects its premisses. (5.575)

And again:

So it appears that this marvelous self-correcting property of Reason, which Hegel made so much of, belongs to every sort of science. . . . (5.579)

There appears to be a bit of trouble here as to whether Peirce has ever read about this principle before or whether Hegel enunciated it, at least in some sense, but the point is clear anyway. The idea seems to be that wherever one commences to reason, no matter if on an entirely false premise, the process of continuing to think long enough will slowly begin to eliminate errors as a self-consistent picture begins to emerge. Peirce's quarrel with Hegel is that Hegel merely follows his own inclinations in his chain of reasoning, which, in his case at least, is very often most fanciful, and ignores the facts of nature, history, and science, in short, facts in general. The scientific method of course has as one of its axioms that one continually checks one's reasoning against experience, and not dictate to the world on the assumption that man's reasoning power is so strong that it can go unhindered from truth to truth. And yet, with this exception duly noted, there is much in common between Hegel's and Peirce's view of the growth of knowledge: Reality is a seamless, internally related, growing whole, which the mind knows by a process of widening the circumference of knowledge – rather than by deducing bits of information in a line leading down from first principles. (Though Hegel must be thought of as using a pseudo-deductive method, it has little in common with mathematical or logical deduction). The image of a circle is here very helpful – a circle which grows by gradually and often imperceptibly filling in gaps of ignorance by creative leaps of inference, in much the same way that a jig-saw puzzle is gradually put together, except there are no outer bounds – but neither is there *a* foundation piece: any place will do to start. One could easily argue, if one wished, that it is impossible in principle to put a jig-saw puzzle together since there are an infinite number of possible ways one might unsuccessfully attempt to piece together any two pieces (there are an infinite number of points on the circumference of each of the two pieces). On this point Whitehead gave William James the credit for discovering "intuitively the great truth with which modern logic is now wrestling" – "that every finite set of premises must indicate notions which are excluded from its direct purview." [8] This remarks seems to be pointing to the problem of trying to see any part of our knowledge as a self-contained whole, when in fact every "part," even, say, Euclid's geometry, is radically interwined with the whole in a web-like or organic fashion,[9] with the result that the intelligibility of every idea depends upon understanding all the ideas closely related to it, and understanding all the ideas closely related to *them,* and so on, *ad infinitum.*

It is impossible to overestimate the importance of this whole point in Peirce's thinking, though it is not something he repeated a great deal. Still, if this viewpoint is substantially accurate, how much of modern philosophy

[8] Alfred North Whitehead, *Modes of Thought* (New York: The Macmillan Co., 1938), pp. 2, 4.
[9] Whitehead gave lavish praise to James for this and other discoveries, not realizing how much James was in debt to Peirce. Cf. Max H. Fisch, *op. cit.,* p. 4.

is undermined – and how many of its puzzles and enigmas vanish! I say "modern," not meaning by that any particular reference to some of the extraordinary sects in modern philosophy, nor meaning particularly to exclude ancient philosophy, since it is clear that what has been said is applicable to much ancient thought, but rather meaning to emphasize the "classical" philosophers generally from Descartes down, and including most of the moderns.

If Peirce's view is correct, no one need fear to tackle any problem for fear of not knowing how to start or for fear of starting from the wrong assumptions. If reasoning tends to grow and correct itself as it goes along, the thing to do is to start. Peirce says that the phenomenon of self-correction "is a property so deeply saturating [inquiry's] inmost nature that it may truly be said that there is but one thing needful for learning the truth, and that is a hearty and active desire to learn what is true." (5.582) This is not to say that a lot of effort might not be wasted in starting off from totally erroneous assumptions, or that shrewd and careful planning of approach is not very valuable, but merely to say that in the last analysis it is dispensable. The "first rule of logic," the "life of science," however, is this: that one love the truth! (*Cf.* 1.135 and 1.235) From this all else follows.

None of this should be taken to imply that the truth is easy to come by – far from it – but what it does imply is very significant, namely, that effort toward finding it is sure to be rewarded to a degree and at last, *and this is the death of scepticism.* Even in a science, or, if one prefers, a discipline, as abstruse and as wracked by internal wars as philosophy, there has been some slight progress through the years if it consists in nothing more than the elimination of some of the more incredible alternatives. And every man's labor has contributed to this progress, perhaps not least of all those who have elaborated to their most unbelievable conclusions those systems now universally rejected.

2. *Fallibilism*

Nature cannot be cheated. If thought has this wonderful property of being self-corrective, it has also a *corresponding drawback*, and that is that thought is not, in principle, an infallible process. Errors may creep in. And this truth is as basic to epistemology and all philosophy as the first truth is, with as many far-reaching implications. The first of these implications is this:

Demonstrative proof is not to be thought of. The demonstrations of the metaphysicians are all moonshine. (1.7)

And again,

Religious infallibilism, caught up in the current of the times shows symptoms
of declaring itself to be only practically speaking infallible; and when it has
thus once confessed itself subject to gradations, there will remain over no
relic of the good old tenth-century infallibilism, except that of the infallible
scientists. . . . (1.8)
Though infallibility in scientific matters seems to me irresistibly comical, I
should be in a sad way if I could not retain a high respect for those who lay
claim to it, for they comprise the greater part of the people who have any
conversation at all. When I say they lay claim to it, I mean they assume the
functions of it quite naturally and unconsciously. The full meaning of the
adage *Humanum est errare*, they have never waked up to. In those sciences
of measurement which are the least subject to error – metrology, geodesy, and
metrical astronomy – no man of self-respect ever now states his results,
without affixing to it its *probable error*; and if this practice is not followed
in other sciences it is because in those the probable errors are too vast to be
estimated. (1.9)

As a result of this small principle of fallibilism one is freed of the necessity
to go ever inward in the futile search for indubitable truths. One can then
in all good conscience look out toward the real world and the world of
common sense without the fear that a list of *conceivable* objections has to
be taken with morbid seriousness. Fallibilism is a "revolutionary" doctrine, says Buchler! [10] "All my philosophy," says Peirce, "has grown from
fallibilism!" (1.14) Even allowing for hyperbole, we are on what was, for
Peirce, very important ground.

For the purpose of making crystal-clear how vast a significance the
doctrine of fallibilism has, as well as for the purpose of raising some other
interesting points, consider now how the doctrine applies to Hume and
Kant.

Concerning Hume, it is quite easy to see how a desire for perfect certainty can make one a sceptic, just as a too overweening desire for all the
money in the world would likely render a man a pauper before his ad-
ventures were over. Hume has given a very good definition of what constitutes scepticism which is particularly interesting when viewed from
Peircean principles:

But that all [Berkeley's] arguments, though otherwise intended, are in reality,
merely sceptical, appears from this, *that they admit of no answer and produce
no conviction*. Their only effect is to cause that momentary amazement and
irresolution and confusion, which is the result of scepticism.[11]

[10] Justus Buchler, *Charles Peirce's Empiricism* (London: Kegan, Paul, Trench, Trubner and Co., Ltd., 1939), p. 177.
[11] David Hume, "An Equiry Concerning Human Understanding," *The English*

The interesting question to raise here is this: was Hume himself a sceptic? If the sceptical arguments "do not produce conviction" – as indeed it is easy to agree they do not – does one *believe* them? It is a contradiction in terms. The fact that Hume could only "believe" his doctrines when isolated from the world in his study, the fact that "nature overcomes all doubts" ought, perhaps, have given Hume reason to believe in the possibility of his having somewhere made a serious error of approach. It is interesting, this admission that sceptical arguments produce no conviction, for ordinarily one says of other such arguments that they are no good. But Hume would have been insulted if anyone else had said that of his efforts.

But now consider some of his specific points:

Hume employs three arguments against the reliability of reason, and this desire for certainty is at the root of two of them. First is the argument that if reason is doubted initially, there is no way to justify it except by a reasoning process which is suspect according to the original doubt. The remedy for this must be, it appears, to refrain from making the original doubt, which in any case can hardly be more than a paper doubt, but rather to jump *in medias res,* to break radically into this vicious circle with a bold, if, *for the moment,* ungrounded, hypothesis.[12] Second is Hume's argument that reason leads to contradictions.[13] But this argument, at least as developed by Hume, is unsuccessful, because Hume thought the notion of infinity was contradictory, which is not necessarily the case. But the third argument is the one important for our discussion here, and that is that if, in any given case of reasoning, the possibility of error is acknowledged, one is only dealing with a probability, and the conclusion that it is a probability is itself another such probable conclusion and so on indefinitely. Here, more clearly than anywhere, it is apparent that this desire for certainty, this feeling that a merely probable conclusion is positively worthless, is the root of the trouble. Whenever Hume speaks of knowledge, he always means absolute and certain knowledge. To him there is all the difference in the world between an overwhelmingly high probability and knowledge. "But knowledge and probability are of such contrary and disagreeing natures, that they cannot well run insensibly into each other. . . .[14]

Philosophers from Bacon to Mill, Edwin A. Burtt, ed. (New York: The Modern Library, 1939), p. 682.

[12] See the last chapter for more on this important point.

[13] Hume, *Enquiry,* pp. 683f.

[14] Hume, *Treatise,* p. 181. And cf. Descartes: ". . . I esteemed as well nigh false all that only went as far as being probable." "Discourse on Method." *The European Philosophers from Descartes to Nietzsche,* Monroe C. Beardsley, ed. (New York: The Modern Library, 1969), p. 10.

Paradoxically, here is where Hume and Peirce come to an agreement (and it is not the only place, for they also approach one another on the question of instinct). Hume and Peirce in fact agree that no "knowledge" in Hume's sense exists, i.e., nothing is infallibly certain. All that exists is high probability: but, contrary to Hume, in common language, as well as in pragmatic language, high probability – so high that the human mind is incapable of entertaining a real, living doubt – is called knowledge!

Part of the trouble lies in this, that Hume does not seem to have a feel for the place of hypothesis in human knowledge. Modern science, perhaps under the influence of Hume, has come to feel that knowledge consists more in those things that cannot be disproved than those things, if any, that can. Consider the causal theory of perception. Few notions enjoy more universal assent among ordinary people. But yet it is a theory that is without strict proof. There is here something to be accounted for, namely, the appearance of sensory phenomena before the mind. *Supposing* the existence of an outside world causally related to our mind, are the phenomena than consistently explained thereby? Yes. Is there any known way to disprove the possibility of the existence of this postulated outside world? No. Very well, then, shall we let this theory become knowledge? Granted that this is not the kind of knowledge Hume wanted, and that indeed and in principle it is very greatly inferior to certain knowledge. But grant too that one must have a word to describe the condition of a theory that is in perfect harmony with all of the known facts, that satisfies our sense of relevance, and that cannot be disproved.

But in this case at least there are alternative theories which account for phenomena and fulfill the last named criterion, that is, they are not subject to disproof: there is Descartes' suggestion that a god may put all these notions in our head – similar in fact to Berkeley's theory, and there is also the possibility that the mind imposes all images upon itself as in dreams and madness it shows itself capable of imposing some images upon itself. Both these theories are equally simple and coherent as the external world theory, and perhaps more so. By what conceivable criterion does one pick between the theories?

Hume answers over and over again with what amounts to Peirce's reply, as mentioned above, that one's choice in matters such as this is determined by a "blind and powerful instinct of nature." [15] (But for Peirce, it isn't *blind*!)

This is an amazing outcome. It does not mean that one ignores em-

[15] Hume, *Enquiry*, p. 680.

pirical or rational considerations. To rely solely upon instinct would certainly be a radical repudiation of both the five senses and the mind. Rather one uses reason as far as one can go, provided one does not let it lead one to a conclusion that is impossible to be believed in a living sense. But if one comes at last to alternative theories all acceptable to reason and none of which can be finally disproved with some kind of crucial experiment, then "the sensitive part of our nature" (Hume) can legitimately be called in for decision. This sounds far more radical than it really is. It becomes more acceptable when it is realized how fundamental a role instinct plays in the very process of inventing alternative theories. If the mind must depend upon some "occult" or "creative" power for the invention of theories, it is hardly in any position to object with too much violence if that some faculty must be called in for a final decision -- after the theories have been tested and purified in so far as possible by empirical and rational tests. The matter is perfectly illustrated by the problem of the existence of the external world. No theory could be more logically air-tight than solipsism. Berkeley's theory and the theory of the external world are *at best* equal in simplicity and coherence to solipsism. (I say "at best" because if one takes the maxim that entities are not to be multiplied beyond necessity, solipsism has the best claim to our attention.) But the community settles upon the theory of the external world as, in some sense, the most satisfying and believable. If we can believe for any reason, with Peirce, that our "sensitive nature" is in tune with the universe (and Peirce gives us good reasons for believing so), we can rest content, counting the theory as literally demonstrated – i.e., supported by considerations which satisfy thoroughly.

And finally, on this subject of the demonstrative approach to philosophy, one might examine Kant in the light of Peirce's notions. Kant certainly wished to undermine Humean scepticism, and to do this he looked for certainties, not mere probabilities. At one point he says of our most fundamental notions, the categories, that they "must either be grounded *a priori* in the understanding, or must be entirely given up as a mere phantom of the brain." [16] It is this little "or" which gave rise to Kant's whole system. We may, along with Peirce, view the results of Kant's work as merely a more elaborate form of nominalism (an "anti-metaphysical scepticism," according to Buchler).[17] This might be a profitable line of

[16] I. Kant, *Critique of Pure Reason*, Norman Kemp Smith, trans. (New York: Macmillan and Co., 1961), p. 125.
[17] Buchler, *The Philosophy of Peirce* (New York: Harcourt, Brace, and Co., 1940), p. xi.

investigation, but it would not be an easy one because of the differences in Kant interpretation. On the other hand, it does seem to be true, in general, that if one ignores the "revolution" part of Kant's philosophy, one can detect in Kant some rough parallels with Peirce. The ideas of the understanding and the ideas of pure reason *unify* experience. The mind tries to fit experience into them, in so far as possible. But this is just what Peirce believes in his doctrine of hypothesis. The mind is driven to a *very good* hypothesis such as that of space or time by long experience, and then, out of the force of habit, the mind seeks to make all experience fall under that hypothesis. Thus, for example, in Peirce the mind is driven, just as in Kant, to the idea of God as a great harmonizing hypothesis.

To be sure, the *certainty* that Kant wanted, which, indeed motivated his whole search, is lost on Peirce's view. A man can always *will* to be a sceptic, and sceptics can't be got rid of as Kant wanted to do. But Peirce's whole philosophy can be viewed as an effort to show the sceptic the unreasonableness of his position, and how his problems can, to a very large and satisfying degree, be answered. The search for certainty has proved to be to the modern mind what the search for a method of transforming base metals into gold was to the middle ages – or the search for a perpetual motion machine or an elixir of youth. A futile but natural quest. But the fallacy of the search for certainty is the most pernicious of them all. As Peirce says, *"Approximation must be the fabric out of which our philosophy has to be built."* (1.404, my emph.)

Consider from the standpoint of Peirce's theories the following informal comments of Russell:

On reaching the age of eighty it is reasonable to suppose that the bulk of one's work is done, and that what remains to do will be of less importance. The serious part of my life ever since boyhood has been devoted to two different objects which for a long time remained separate and have only in recent years united into a single whole. I wanted, on the one hand, to find out whether anything could be known; and on the other hand to do whatever might be possible toward creating a happier world. Up to the age of thirty-eight I gave most of my energies to the first of these tasks. I was troubled by skepticism and unwillingly forced to the conclusion that most of what passes for knowledge is open to reasonable doubt. I wanted certainty in the kind of way in which people want religious faith. I thought that certainty is more likely to be found in mathematics than elsewhere. But I discovered that many mathematical demonstrations, which my teachers expected me to accept, were full of fallacies, and that, if certainty were indeed discoverable in mathematics, it would be in a new kind of mathematics, with more solid foundations than those that had hitherto been thought secure. But as the work proceeded, I was continually reminded of the fable about the elephant and the tortoise. Having constructed an elephant upon which the mathematical world could rest, I found the elephant tottering, and proceeded to construct a tortoise to keep the elephant from falling. But the tortoise was no more secure than the elephant, and after some twenty years of very arduous toil, I came to the conclusion that there was nothing more that I could do in the way of making mathematical knowledge indubitable.[18]

And again:

Mill's law of causation is, in fact, only roughly and approximately true in an everyday and unscientific sense. Nevertheless, he thinks it is proved by an inference which elsewhere he considers very shaky; that of induction by simple enumeration. This process is not only shaky, but can be proved quite definitely to lead to false consequences more often than true ones. If you find n objects all of which possess two properties, A and B, and you then find another object possessing the property A, it can easily be proved that it is unlikely to possess the property B. This is concealed from common sense by the fact that our animal propensity toward induction is confined to the sort of the cases in which induction is liable to give correct results. Take the following as an example of an induction which no one would make; all the sheep that Kant ever saw were within ten miles of Konigsberg, but he felt no inclination to induce that all sheep were within ten miles of Konigsberg.

Modern physics does not use induction in the old sense at all. It makes enormous theories without pretending that they are in any exact sense true, and uses them only hypothetically until new facts turn up which require new theories. All that the modern physicist claims for a theory is that it fits the known facts and therefore cannot at present be refuted. The problem of induction in its traditional form has by most theoretical physicists been abandoned as insoluble. I am not by any means persuaded that they are right in this, but I think it is quite definitely demonstrable that the problem is very different from what Mill supposed it to be.[19]

These comments, taken more or less at random from many like them which Russell makes, illustrate, more than any one point, how differently one reads philosophy after seeing things from Peirce's point of view – how pregnant with meaning even the most random philosophical comments can become. In the latter quotation particularly it is interesting to see the way Russell is groping toward the notion of abduction.

3. *Contextualism and Organism.*

Having now discussed in our first section the notion that knowledge is a self-corrective process, and in our second section the concept of fallibilism and the way it points out of philosophical scepticism, we are now pre-

[18] Bertrand Russell, *Portraits from Memory and Other Essays* (New York: Simon and Schuster, 1951), pp. 540f.
[19] *Ibid.*, pp. 125f.

pared to bring all of these ideas together into a harmonized epistemological position. The main point of this position, which is a form of contextualism, is that knowledge grows organically, and that the whole fabric of our mental life is woven together into a network of interdependent, mutually supporting concepts, none of which can be taken as primitive. The elephant supports the tortoise, and the tortoise supports the elephant.

Let us return for a moment to the image of a circle which was used to represent human knowledge. The notion of circularity or of an infinite regress is one that crops up in Peirce every so often and in some way seems to play an important role in his doctrine. At one point Peirce refers to the process of abstraction as the consideration of an operation as itself something to be operated on, as is common in mathematics. (1.83) Immediately it occurs to one that this kind of thing could be done indefinitely. In 6.428 Peirce speaks of the scientific method as itself a scientific result. This too is provocative. Josiah Royce loved to point out instances of thought's "self-transcending quality," as in "the thought of a thought," "the consciousness of self," "loyalty to the ideal of loyalty." [20] Arthur F. Smullyan, in an essay called "Implications of Critical Common-Sensism," [21] has an admirable discussion which relates to this very point – how one can inquire into standards of inquiry:

One cannot surrender the presuppositions of inquiry and retain the perspective in inquiry. If one *will* not distinguish between the valid and invalid, if one *will* not accept the dictates of memory, if one *will* not generalize from the data, if one *will* not infer from the data of sense that there are objective realities, then, though nirvana be achieved, and the achievement be ever so important, such blessedness will be a trance in which all dreams are black.

Genuine inquiry presupposes confidence in the working logic of inquiry, which is not to say that it presupposes confidence in every highly precise logistic formulation or analysis of it. It is central to the doctrine which Peirce called Critical Common-sensism that we distinguish between *logica utens* and *logica docens*. The *logica utens* is our crude, natural, logical wit. It is the complex system of criteria, some of them explicitly grasped, some implicitly employed, by which we determine matters of relevance and consistency. If mathematical logic is not merely an algorithm, if it pretends to be a precise formulation of the validating logical forms, then its consistency must be judged by reference to the more obscurely formulated ideas of validity and consistency which compose the *logica utens* of inquiry.

The suggestion in these remarks is the same as what we have been trying to convey in the image of breaking violently into a circle by what amounts

[20] Cf. Otto F. Kraushaar's essay in Fish, *op. cit.,* p. 191.
[21] Smullyan, "Some Implications of Critical Common-Sensism" in Philip P. Wiener and Frederic H. Young, edd., *Studies in the Philosophy of Charles Sanders Peirce* (Cambridge: Harvard Univ. Press, 1952), pp. 111ff.

to nothing more than an act of *willing*, by trusting thought, at first, without knowing *exactly* why, and perhaps without ever being able to know exactly why. Peirce commends the scholastics for having the good judgment never to question fundamentals: (5.264) And again he says with great emphasis: "The Criticist believes in criticizing first principles, while the Common-sensist thinks such criticism is all nonsense."(5.505) And we might go back several hundred years to that very acute mind, Pascal:

We know truth, not only by the reason, but also by the heart, and it is in the last way that we know first principles, and reason, which has no part in it, tries in vain to impugn them. The skeptics, who have only this for their object, labor to no purpose. We know that we do not dream, and however impossible it is for us to prove it by reason, this inability demonstrates only the weakness of our reason, but not, as they affirm, the uncertainty of all our knowledge. For the knowledge of first principles, as space, time, motion, number, is as sure as any of those which we get from reasoning. And reason must trust these intuitions of the heart, and must base them on every argument. . . . Would to God . . . that we knew everything by instinct and intuition! But nature has refused us this boon. On the contrary, she has given us but very little knowledge of this kind; and all the rest can be acquired only by reasoning.[22]

All of this is nearly pure Peirce. Pascal was making all the right criticisms of Descartes while most philosophers were just beginning the long elaboration of Cartesianism which was to go on for centuries.

And compare on these points Santayana:

Dogma cannot be abandoned; it can only be revised in view of some more elementary dogma which it has not yet occurred to the sceptic to doubt. . . .[23]

[First principles] can never be discovered, if discovered at all, until they have long been taken for granted, and employed in the very investigation which reveals them.[24]

This is circularity certainly, but it is a circle which envelopes the whole of human knowledge. Reality may be thought of as a self-contained whole, and therefore our idea of it, if ever perfected, would be a self-contained whole. The only way to break out of this circle would be to change our mode of being so that our knowledge would be intuitional and not inferential – i.e., to become God!

In another place Peirce makes a clever allusion to this same point

---

[22] Pascal, *Pensees* William F. Trotter, Trans. (N.Y.: Washington Square Press, 1965), pp. 85f.

[23] George Santayana, *Scepticism and Animal Faith* (New York: Charles Scribner's Sons, 1923), p. 8.

[24] *Ibid.*, p. 2.

(1.147; 1.151). He develops his argument that there is no way for the human mind to reach perfect certitude or exactitude. He says, "... the doctrine is true; – without claming absolute certainty for it, it is *substantially* unassailable." The problem which Peirce so tantalizingly raises in this sentence is that it invites us to stand back and view human knowledge as a whole and then make some statement about it, which statement will be true of itself as a part of human knowledge. What is it to say that "we never can be absolutely sure of anything?" If we can not be sure of *that,* then it is possible that, in some rare case, we can be absolutely sure of something. The circularity seems to be hopeless.

But this phenomenon is far from unique. This same type of difficulty is encountered in the case of defining words. The dictionary either uses synonyms or expresses the thought in a simple sentence or sentences. It is a wonder indeed that no sceptic has applied himself to the proof that no one can possibly learn any word whatever, since words are all defined by other words. To say that one can learn words by being *shown,* raises interesting points. In the first place, this is the point of pragmatism. Everyone realizes how easy it is to become lost in a morass of words, and it is feared that much philosophy has done that. So the remedy is to take complex words or ideas and conceive of what real differences they would make or what their "upshot" would be, to relate them, if not to reality, at least to our experience. In this way one certainly has the advantage of breaking out of the circle of synonyms, but it is not at all evident that one has broken out of a circle altogether. Perhaps at best one has broken out of a small one into a larger one.

The story of Helen Keller may hold a clue for this mystery. As a little child she went for many years without having any opportunity to learn what a word was. Finally her tutor began to spell into Helen's hand the names of various objects. This was done for a long period, and met with the blankest incomprehension on Helen's part. Virtually the only contact the outside world had with Helen was though the pleasure-pain principle. In this way she was taught some elementary principles of behavior, but as yet she had no conception of what a word was or of the notion that thoughts could be got across to other people's minds by other than brute means. According to the story, one day Helen's tutor spelled the word "water" into her hand while both of their hands were under the water flowing out of a pump. In a flash of insight – *an abduction if ever there was one* – Helen saw what all of this spelling was about. Immediately she ran about grasping objects and pounding on objects not ceasing till its name had been spelled into her hand. Her desire to learn names became insatiable, and, of course, having caught on to the principle, having broken into the circle, learning the whole language was merely a matter of time and work.

This story makes almost irresistible the suggestion that language is a closed, or nearly closed circle. One gets the point of what language is about in a flash. No one can help a person get the point of what it is all about, except most indirectly, nor, in all probability, does one get the point gradually, even in the case of little children. Rather, if it is an abduction, it comes like a flash. Things are said to "dawn" on people. The same kind of phenomenon can be seen in many other cases. For example, the point of a geometrical proof often comes home in this same kind of burst of insight – essentially the same kind of burst of insight that occurred to the inventer of the proof.

The same kind of sceptical argument which asserts that men know nothing, and even if they did they could not know that they knew it, and even if they knew it and knew that they knew it, they could not prove it to anyone else, could just as well be applied to the science of cryptology. Here are some documents in a dead language, or in a live tongue but put into a highly complex code. How will it ever be possible to translate them? Those addicted to the deductive method will insist on being given a lexicon or a key to the code, and will confidently allege that without this kind of rock-bottom foundation nothing can ever be known for certain about what the documents say, and not being known with certainty, nothing will be known at all. But codes and languages *are* broken.

Cryptography is a science of deduction (sic) and controlled experiment; hypotheses are formed, tested and often discarded. But the residue which passes the test grows and grows till finally there comes a point when the experimenter feels solid ground beneath his feet: his hypotheses cohere, and fragments of sense emerge from their camouflage. The code "breaks." Perhaps this is best defined as the point when the likely leads appear faster than they can be followed up. It is like the initiation of a chain-reaction in atomic physics; once the critical threshold is passed, the reaction propagates itself.[25]

The important thing to observe in these remarks is the fact that knowledge *grows and grows*, and begins to *hold together, cohere,* and finally it begins to harden and solidify and to become "solid ground" under the feet of the investigator. Every piece is dubitable; nothing serves as a sure foundation piece. But the *whole*, unlike the parts, becomes sure and

[25] John Chadwick, *The Decipherment of Linear B*, quoted in I. M. Copi, *Introduction to Logic*, (New York: Macmillan, 1961), p. 342.

solid and in the psychological sense, "certain." [26] The scientific method itself teaches us that a conclusion can be far more certain than any of the facts which support it. (5.237)

Surely it is clear that language at least does not rest on some kind of indubitable foundation, or a kind of axiomatic base. Nor does one have to learn it in any given order.[27] The important thing is that the main point be understood, and any word or words that are handy and easy will do to begin. And, true enough, once one has a toe-hold on the language, the rest can come much more easily. Also one need not worry too much about the niceties of grammar as long as communication is unhindered. The grammar will take care of itself after a while. Misunderstandings will tend to be corrected with usage.

Now it would be hard to say how far these facts concerning verbal, spoken language would legitimately be said to represent or parallel the pattern of cognitive processes in general. There may be essential differences, but even so the suggestion of what is meant by saying human knowledge is in a circle may be roughly true. It does not have an axiomatic basis, it grows by abductive leaps, it is self-corrective, and, in all probability, efforts to transcend it – to look upon it as a whole – will be paradoxical, (but not necessarily on that account futile or false when correctly understood). This is perhaps another way of saying that we are not God, or that we cannot get out of our own skins.

Also this line of thought suggests that knowledge is all interconnected and of a piece. Imagine the task of trying to define a word to someone who continually asks the meaning of each new word you use in your definition. One would soon be led to outline the whole spectrum of human knowledge, and would indeed soon enough come to its boundaries. (Example: What is *color*? Color is "a sensation evoked as a response to the stimulation of the eye and its attached nervous mechanisms by radiant energy of certain wave lengths and intensities." (Webster's New Collegiate Dictionary). But what is: a sensation, a response, a stimulation, an eye, being attached, a nerve, a mechanism, energy, radiant energy, a wave,

---

[26] Compare on this point Brand Blanshard's statement of the coherence theory: "Fully coherent knowledge would be knowledge in which every judgment entailed and was entailed by the rest of the system." *The Nature of Thought* (London, 1939), Vol. II, p. 264 as quoted in S. Korner *Conceptual Thinking* (N.Y.: Dover Pub. Inc., 1959), p. 204.

[27] Boswell once asked Johnson what is was best to teach children first. Johnson replied, "Sir, it is no matter what you teach them first, any more than what leg you shall put into your breeches first. Sir, you may stand disputing which is best to put in first, but in the mean time, your breech is bare. Sir, while you are considering which of two things you should teach your child first, another boy has learnt them both."

length, intensity? How quickly indeed we arrive at the limits of human knowledge with just one simple word! I say "the limits" because I doubt if anyone has a very clear idea of what energy is – to take one thing on the list. Or try the game on the word "theosophy," and consider all the italicized words: "Alleged *knowledge* of *God* and of the *world* as *related* to God *obtained* by *direct mystical insight* or by *philosophical speculation* or by a *combination* of both." (*Ibid.*)

According to Peirce's theory, a word takes on greater depth and richness the more one learns, and particularly as the new knowledge is closely related to the word in question. He says, "How much more the word *electricity* means now than it did in the time [of] Hipparchus." (7.587) And not only do *individual concepts* depend for their meaning and significance on all other concepts, but *the method of reasoning itself can be refined and improved the more it is understood and used.* Science itself, more than anything else, may be said to be correct method. And the paradox is that this method is itself a result of science. Whitehead says that the greatest discovery of the 19th century was the discovery of the method of discovery itself.[28] The better method one has for unearthing truths, the faster knowledge is expanded; and the more the method is used, the more refined and improved it becomes. This circle is open to sceptical objections, once again, but they all betray the false basis of scepticism. The fact that science discovers its own method, and progresses even more rapidly by the use of this method does not undermine both science and the method but to the contrary is a case again of "organism" – or mutual help through mutual support. Spinoza supplies us with another example of this same kind of phenomenon in the case of tool-making (and this from a devotee of the deductive method if ever there was one!):

The matter stands on the same footing as the making of material tools, which might be argued about in a similar way. For, in order to work iron, a hammer is needed, and the hammer cannot be forth-coming unless it has been made; but, in order to make it, there was need of another hammer and other tools, and so on to infinity. We might thus vainly endeavor to prove that men have no power of working iron. But as men at first made use of the instruments supplied by nature to accomplish very easy pieces of workmanship, laboriously and imperfectly, and then, when these were finished, wrought other things more difficult with less labor and greater perfection; and so gradually mounted from the simplest operations to the making of tools, and from the making of tools to the making of more complex tools, and fresh feats of

---

[28] Alfred North Whitehead, *Science and the Modern World* (New York: the New American Library, 1948), p. 91. This is a bit of an exaggeration, for we cannot say that the method of discovery has been discovered. We could more truly say that it has been discovered that there is no *mechanical* method of discovery.

workmanship, till they arrived at making, with small expenditure of labor, the vast number of complicated mechanisms which they now possess. So in like manner, the intellect, by its native strength, makes for itself intellectual instruments, whereby it acquires strength for performing other intellectual operations, and from these operations gets again fresh instruments, or the power of pushing its investigations further, and thus gradually proceeds till it reaches the summit of wisdom.[29]

Knowledge is thus a highly complex and interrelated affair. It is not stretching things to imagine that, just as every atom exerts its force throughout the whole universe, each additional bit of insight clarifies and amplifies to a degree all the related concepts, and to a lesser degree all concepts related to them and so on. It might be added that all of this applies equally to the pragmatic definition of a word. One can think of possible sensible effects, but these need to be thoroughly understood in all their completeness, and this is an endless job. Buchler puts this whole matter very well when he says that, for Peirce, thought "is not a granular succession, but a web of continuously related signs. This is really the heart of fallibilism. All science, all significant inquiry is a web with indefinite frontiers." [30]

There might seem to be some conflict in Peirce's system between what he says about the continuous nature of sign activity and the fact of sudden abductive "insight." This, however, would be a misunderstanding easily cleared up. The flow of signs is always continuous, even during abduction. An abduction is "sudden" or comes in a "flash" only relatively speaking. While seeking a probable hypothesis the mind somehow ranges over the possibilities until it hits upon a good hypothesis which it presents to the consciousness – but the "hitting upon" or the "flash" with which the idea comes before the attention is only sudden in the psychological sense – not the metaphysical sense; in the same way a sound may be said to be "sudden," but still the perception of the sound has been a continuous affair.

Moreover, there is no reason to suppose there is a real conflict between Peirce's idea that knowledge is supported by many threads of inference and his contention that it is of the nature of an "insight." This "insight" is not a Cartesian "intuition." It is merely the mind's coming to view its data from a particularly fruitful or unifying standpoint. This "viewing" is itself

[29] B. Spinoza, *On the Improvement of the Understanding* in *Spinoza Selections*, John Wild, ed. (New York: Charles Scribner's Sons, 1930), pp. 10f. But is there a "summit?"
[30] Justus Buchler, ed., *The Philosophy of Peirce* (New York: Harcourt and Co., 1940), p. xii.

continuous. The insight is *justified* partly by the multiplicity of the considerations that point to it.

In summary, we may say that although there is much about these matters which is not at all clear, Peirce's position, if generally correct, *inclines* one to believe that he was right in his attack on Descartes' view of knowledge. It inclines one to believe that rather than waiting for knowledge to be infallibly grounded, one ought to jump *in medias res* [31] and start thinking in the hope and expectation that erroneous presuppositions will be found out eventually. It inclines us to trust that central fabric of our opinions which has been weaved out of years of experience, and which has become, not merely a *tissue* of inference, but a strong cloth of inferences so interconnected that it is solid enough to stand on. Here such things are meant as the existence of the outside world, the existence of "psyches" in other people, the orderliness of nature and so forth. It is no mean thing in philosophy to have a credible proof for the existence of the outside world. Ever since Descartes, philosophy has been trying to climb out of that solipsistic hole he dug, and with a notable lack of success, and with agreement too that Descartes' own way was fallacious. Perhaps now the problem of the existence of the outside world can be de-"bracketed." [32]

Every thought, therefore, every step of reasoning, unless it is a mere free play of association, implies laws or rules of good reasoning. Even thinking or examining those rules of good reasoning has to be done in the light of even more fundamental standards of reasoning. Thus every controlled thought or step of reasoning presupposes an uncriticized network of presuppositions or "premisses" as Peirce calls them. One is therefore faced with either trusting this fabric of premises or rejecting it. If one pretends to reject it, he cannot pretend to do so for good *reasons*, because the existence of good reasons is what is being rejected. It is strange that most sceptics have tried to project an image of sweet reasonableness, when, by their doctrine, they admit themselves to be unreasonable. But it is not so strange when one realizes that no one is a real sceptic in the sense that he is able to maintain a "living" doubt of reason or of any of the other fundamentals of common sense.

---

[31] Cf. Santayana: "A philosopher is compelled to follow the maxim of epic poets and to plunge *in medias res.*" *Op. cit.,* p. 1.

[32] Phenomenologists perpetuate Descartes' error of wanting to do philosophy by the geometrical method. But they can't even deal with the problem of the existence of the outside world – they can't get off the ground!

CHAPTER IV

CONCRETE REASONABLENESS:
COOPERATION BETWEEN REASON AND INSTINCT

Peirce was not a "one-idea'd" philosopher. He is most famous for his development of the idea of pragmatism, but this was one idea among many
for Peirce. As Peirce continues to become more widely known, the recognition grows that he had original and incisive things to say on almost all
of the most interesting philosophical questions. In this chapter we will see
Peirce at his best, making many creative suggestions which bear upon most
difficult questions. First we will discuss the basic role which our primitive
instincts play in the reasoning process, particularly as our instinct guides
the abductive process. Then we will try to show where instinct should be
trusted and where it should not be trusted, by way of balancing the
emphasis which Peirce places on instinct.

A. ABDUCTION IS INFERENCE GUIDED BY NATURE'S HAND

The problem of this first division may be summarized in the following
question: How do people *ever* get a correct theory? This indeed is a problem though it may not appear to be one at first sight. But when it has been
reflected upon, this problem of the origin of creative new hypotheses has
puzzled and agonized many thinkers. Sometimes it seems that the best we
can say is that the creative man is just a "genius." In this manner, we
name the phenomenon, but shed no light on it. It is Peirce's merit again
that not only has he suggested a highly plausible hypothesis on this matter,
but that this hypothesis is rooted and grounded in his system as a whole.
It is not by any means a detached suggestion, but one that relates to all the
most vital parts of his system – to his doctrines of evolution, synechism,
abduction and inference, and to what he says about theory and practice,
science and religion. It is a suggestion of the first magnitude, philosophically speaking.

   To elaborate on the nature of this problem briefly, there seems to be a large, indeed infinite, number of wrong theories which might be proposed to explain any given phenomenon. How does the mind ever guess the right one, or even a partially right one? How is the mind able, with such a sure feel for reality, to dismiss uncounted irrelevancies which might erroneously be thought to bear on any given problem? How does the atomic physicist know to ignore the fluctuations of the stock market, or the biography of a long deceased hero of history? To say that those things are relevant which have some kind of causal connection upon the phenomenon in question, is merely to put the question in another form. In what consists causal connection? Constant connection? Clearly not. Physical proximity? Even more clearly not. At least it is easy to think of cases where these two features are present without any apparent causal connection. In fact, it is just another way to express the problem to ask: How do we know where to look for causes and where not to look?

To say, as has been said above, that the mind looks for a unifying, harmonizing principle, is really again only to put the problem another way, or, more likely, to conceal the problem with high-sounding words like "unifying" and "harmonizing." For the real problem lies in the fact that phenomena can be unified in all sorts of ways. Fluctuations on the stock market might accidentally have a correlation with data gathered by an atomic physicist. Picasso can bring unity to a scene of nature – a unity as real as the physicist's – but not relevant in the least to the "truth" about physical nature (*Cf.* 1.303). Unity can be had easily. But what is hard to come by is to see the *real* interconnections, the unity, not merely of our own creative fancy, but the unity employed by nature herself.

The following puzzle is, I fancy, a good illustration of the problem under discussion. There is a series of infinite length composed of English letters beginning OTTFF. . . . What is the "real" ordering principle behind the construction of this series? How would a machine go about solving this problem, supposing it had all the information at its disposal that I did when working on the problem? It appears that it would have blindly to go through every conceivable possibility. But there are an infinite number of possibilities. For example, here is one wrong solution to the problem: "O" is the fifteenth letter in the alphabet; "T" is the twentieth; "F" is the sixth. Perhaps the series is constructed by dropping back one letter, and the next group is NSSEE, and so on indefinitely, going back to "Z" after "A." This certainly brings a unity to the problem and is a *possible* solution. But perhaps the rule is more complex. Here is another wrong solution: Perhaps these letters are the initial letters to the first words in the first book in the upper, right-hand corner of the bookcase in my study, and the next letters are the initial letters to the succeeding words in that book, and so on through that book and all the other books in the bookcase, and then repeat the series. Or perhaps the rule is similar to that but even more complex. Perhaps the rule has something to do with the shape of the letters. There is no end to wrong theories, and to wrong ways to impose a unity on the series.

Now, by wrong theories, I naturally mean theories other than the one that the originator of the puzzle had in mind. As stated above, the puzzle is so vague that OTTFF .... repeated indefinitely would satisfy the conditions. A machine would give this as a possible answer, unless it could somehow *sense the futility and inappropriateness* of such an answer. The same is true of the other proposed answers. But what we are really looking for is the unity that imposes, or tends to impose, *itself on us,* not we on it – and this is in harmony with Peirce's definition of the real – that which *forces itself on us.*

In my own case, I was unable to think of the answer to the problem for two days or so, when it came to me in a flash one morning as I just waked up.

There are in fact *two* interesting problems here: first is the problem of how the mind could seek out an appropriate answer among all the irrelevant possible answers, and second, how to explain the fact that once the real answer comes to a person, he *knows* and senses that this is the correct answer – and has no real need to check up with anyone. His confidence is complete. When it is understood whence this confidence comes, one has a real insight into Peirce's theory and also a confirmation of it.

The only way to express Peirce's theory is to say that the person who solves the problem has enough insight into human psychology to know or sense or feel that the correct answer is the kind of answer that makes the puzzle significantly interesting to other people. The subconscious hones in on "interesting" solutions, and ignores the vast quantity of possible and *ad hoc* solutions.

How a machine could answer this puzzle other than by going blindly through every conceivable possibility – and whether it could do it even this way in anything less than a short eternity, I do not know. And how it could recognize the significant answer when it found it, is the second problem.

But to say the mind can solve such a problem (and problems of science in general are included) is not to say *how* it does so. Peirce's answer to this problem is vague, but perhaps as good a first step as has ever been suggested. Peirce's answer would be, in the case of the puzzle, that my mind is kin to the minds of other people and therefore tends to work in the same way. Common sense certainly supports the notion that human minds are similiar in essentials. But there is the old saw about how one can be sure that my perception of the color red is at all like the other person's. A little reflection shows there is no way of knowing for certain and it is easy to come to some sort of sceptical conclusion. Peirce cites the case of the blind man who had surmised from things he had heard that the color red must be something like the blare of a trumpet. Peirce thinks that this is somehow a remarkably accurate statement and that is shows the "community of feelings" that people share. Of course it proves nothing, since a man who saw red as a shade of orange might well have something of the same quality of sensation. If one insists upon a demonstration, nothing would be easier than to reject this form of argument and lapse into scepticism. James says that the assumption that men's feelings are similar is the "simplest hypothesis that meets the case," though, "as a matter of fact we never *are* sure of it." [1] If one wants to be sceptical, one can ask, as Peirce pointed out (1.314*ff.*) whether even in the case of the same individual his perception of red is the same today as it was yesterday, or is the same this moment as it was the last. This is exactly the same question in principle as the former one, but our belief in memory is much too strong to be overcome by this sceptical approach.

So the notion that human psychology has a certain common nature, besides being believed by everyone anyway, is open to a philosophical defense. In the case, however, of the discovery of *physical* theories (as contrasted to man-made problems such as our puzzle), the assertion, the proposed answer as to how we come to true theories, is more interesting – namely, that the true physical theories are sought out by the mind with some degree of accuracy because the mind is somehow in tune with nature and in harmony with it, just as it is in tune with other minds.

In examining the reasonings of those physicists who gave to modern science the initial propulsion which has insured its healthful life ever since, we are struck with the great, though not absolutely decisive, weight they allowed to instinctive judgments. Galileo appeals to *il lume naturale* at the most critical stages of his reasoning. Kepler, Gilbert, and Harvey – not to speak of Copernicus – substantially rely upon an inward power, not sufficient to reach the truth by itself, but yet supplying an essential factor to the influences carrying their minds to the truth. (1.80)

---

[1] James, "The Function of Cognition," in *Pragmatism,* p. 211f.

When the mind faces a problem it begins to search according to rules of its own – ignoring data that have no possible relevance – looking where it knows, – How?, by sentiment, by feeling, by instinct? – a possible answer may lay. This process, of course, is so often accomplished subconsciously, as the history of great insights testifies, that it is hard to imagine how else the mind could do this, if something like Peirce's theory were not true.

> ... the categories suggest our looking for a synthetizing law; and this we find in the power of assimilation, incident to which is the habit-taking faculty. This is all the categories pretend to do. They suggest a way of think- ing; and the possibility of science depends upon the fact that human thought necessarily partakes of whatever character is diffused through the whole universe, and that its natural modes have some tendency to be the modes of action of the universe. (1.351)

This last sentence summarizes Peirce's theory very well, especially in its suggestion that the human mind is as much a part of nature as is anything else, and therefore can be assumed to be not totally foreign to nature's ways and not dependent upon purely blind or fortuitous stabs in its efforts to comprehend nature.

Concerning this theory, Bertrand Russell has made these brief remarks:

> [Peirce] holds – and I confess that an examination of scientific inference has made me feel the force of this view – that man is adapted, by his congenital constitution, to the apprehension of natural laws which cannot be proved by experience, although experience is in conformity with them. "The chicken you say pecks by instinct. But if you are going to think every poor chicken endowed with an innate tendency towards a positive truth, why should you think that to man alone this gift is denied?" This is an important question, to which I do not know the answer.[2]

Buchler has pointed out that Mach, independently of Peirce, came to much the same kind of conclusion with regard to the role of instinct in the abductive process. For Mach, our instinctive feel for nature always pre- ceeds a scientific unravelment of it. Instinct is very fallible in its suggesting of hypotheses, but it serves a crucial function in *guiding* the mind, putting it on the scent. Instinct is acquired in the development of the race. These are all exact parallels of Peirce's thought.[3]

There just does not seem to be any plausible escape from the notion that the mind *does* know by some "inward power" to reject some hypotheses utterly and look with favor on others.

[2] In the "Foreword" to Feibleman, *op. cit.*, p. xvi.
[3] Buchler, *Peirce's Empiricism*, p. 142n.1.

If you ask an investigator why he does not try this or that wild theory, he will say, "It does not seem *reasonable*." It is curious that we seldom use this word where the strict logic of our procedure is clearly seen. We do [not] say that a mathematical error is not reasonable. We call that opinion reasonable whose only support is instinct. . . . (5.174) (Brackets in the text.)

Now this theory, of the mind's in-tune-ment with nature, is at the basis of much of what Peirce says about metaphysics and religion, and its implications for all these areas of thought are truly enormous, as one can sense almost immediately.

B. EVOLUTION AND CRITICAL-COMMONSENSISM

Peirce, being as he was, a convinced evolutionist, finds it plausible to account for the mind's kinship with nature by pointing to man's roots in nature as a creature of nature. (But man's mind is also in continuous connection with God's, as we see below (6.307)).

In Peirce's essay on "Evolutionary Love" (6.287ff.) he examines various theories of evolution with an eye toward showing that the principles of man's physical development are the same principles underlying man's intellectual and spiritual development, and in particular showing that no simple mechanism will suffice, but rather that there is a need for such concepts as growth, sympathy and love.

Peirce suggests that there are three types of evolutions – evolution by chance, by mechanical necessity, and evolution by what he calls "love." He points out against Lamarckism that "direct endeavor can achieve almost nothing." "It is as easy by taking thought to add a cubit to one's stature as it is to produce an idea acceptable to any one of the Muses by merely straining for it before it is ready to come." (6.301) Rather, "the deeper workings of the spirit take place in their own slow way, without our connivance." (*Ibid.*)

Those parts of the mind which have mastered their tasks sink into a lethargic habit, but "a succession of surprises wonderfully brightens the ideas." (*Ibid.*) "Thus, the first step in the Lamarckian evolution of mind is the putting of sundry thoughts into situations in which they are free to play." (*Ibid.*) But the evolution of mind proceeds under the guidance of the hand of love:

The agapastic development of thought is the adoption of certain mental tendencies, not altogether heedlessly, as in tychism ["chance-ism"], nor quite blindly by the mere force of circumstances or of logic, as in anacasm [mechanism], but by an immediate attraction for the idea itself, whose nature is divined before the mind possesses it, by the power of sympathy, that is, by virtue of the continuity of mind; and this mental tendency may be of three varieties, ... (6.307)

This development may take place in the mental life of the whole community or society, or in the mental life of an individual under the strong influence of social circumstances, or, finally. "... it may affect an individual, independently of his human affections, by virtue of an attraction it exercises upon his mind, even before he has comprehended it. This is the phenomenon which has been well called the *divination* of genius; for it is due to the continuity between the man's mind and the Most High." (*Ibid.*) On the other hand, Peirce adds, "I doubt if any of the great discoveries ought, properly, to be considered as altogether individual achievements; and I think many will share this doubt. Yet, if not, what an argument for the continuity of mind, and for agapasticism is here!" (6.317)

Thus, Peirce's doctrine of instinct is tied by the closest bonds to his deepest metaphysical doctrines. The continuity of signs, of all mental life, as it flows and tends to organize itself under more general heads, the evolution of physical laws, biological laws, and the life of the mind – all this tied together in a very provocative package.

The contents of this package, the general expression of all these phenomena is the growth of "concrete reasonableness" throughout the whole cosmos. Under the head of "concrete reasonableness" there are three or four succinct expressions of Peirce's doctrine from his own pen which are worth quoting:

Almost everybody will now agree that the ultimate good lies in the evolutionary process in some way. If so, it is not in individual reactions in their segregation, but in something general or continuous. Synechism is founded on the notion that the coalescence, the becoming continuous, the becoming governed by laws, the becoming instinct with general ideas, are but phases of one and the same process of growth of reasonableness. (5.4)

And in another place he ties this doctrine down to his notion of pragmaticism:

Accordingly, the pragmaticist does not make the *summum bonum* to consist in action, but makes it to consist in that process of evolution whereby the existent comes more and more to embody those generals which were just now said to be *destined*, which is what we strive to express in calling them *reasonable*. In its higher stages, evolution takes place more and more largely through self-control, and this gives the pragmaticist a sort of justification for making the rational purport to be general. (5.433)

This theory of the gradual growth of the truth as an aspect of the growth of concrete reasonableness, and instinct's place in this theory, raises very difficult and interesting questions relating to the old debate concerning innate knowledge, or *a priori* knowledge, and the blank tablet theory. Peirce's theory is something new in that he supposes an *innate tendency towards truth,* quite different from Leibniz, Locke, or Kant. His theory has not a little to commend it. The mind certainly comes into the world *pre-adapted to a world like ours.* It is *ready,* with a highly sensitive and elaborate apparatus, to see, hear, feel, taste, and smell, – and that before having done any of these things. Might it not also be *ready,* in a weaker sense, to learn the law of gravitation and other scientific truths? This is not a fanciful theory. How long would the human organism have had to wait to learn about light and electromagnetic phenomena in general if it had not been equipped with the complex and delicate structure which forms the eye and the related parts of the brain and nervous structure?

But as interesting and stimulating as this theory is, it leads to most difficult questions. (Rather, this is an added virtue of the theory). Consider, for example, all the knowledge of physics, and of aero-dynamic theory in particular, which is implicit in the bird's ability to fly – and not merely to fly in a simple more or less straight path as airplanes usually do, but to execute highly complex aerial gymnastics (as when pursuing an insect). Consider, for that matter, all that the fertilized egg must already "know" about light and color in order to make an eye. True, the information in neither case is explicit in the form of conscious knowledge, but it is not any less real information for that. Information may be stored in natural objects in precisely the same way it is stored on computer tapes but of course not consciously in either case.

But pressing the thought further, ordinary language does not hesitate to say that a bird knows how to fly, just as a man knows how to walk or run or swim or skate. A man knows how to skate when he can move effectively on skates, and not only when he can analyze in an explicit way the dynamics of the roller skate under all sorts of complex pressures. But how far can one follow the dictates of common usuage in analyzing a philosophical question? Plants certainly turn to the light, but one can hardly say that they know to. And this has nothing to do with the fact that they are not self-conscious, but only with the fact that they are not conscious at all.

Consider another provocative example: there are any number of people who know no music theory of any kind, who can play no instrument and read no notes. And yet, they can hear a tune and immediately they can whistle the melody back. To whistle different notes clearly requires an ability to make a rather fine adjustment in the many muscles that control the cheeks and lips. And to whistle a coherent tune requires the ability to go unerringly from tone to tone, sometimes, in complicated melodies, making an interval between notes that very seldom follow one another, and doing so in a complex rhythmic pattern. If the person were asked to sound the interval between, say, a *re* and the *me* in the next octave up, he would be unable to do so – at least not without figuring it out, but if such an interval occurred in the melody he just heard, he could do it easily. Now in what sense does such a person *know* music? The majority of people perhaps fit into just such a description as this – knowing no theory, but able to sing or whistle a tune. In one sense, surely, their knowledge is extensive – for it requires a complex series of muscular adjustments to whistle. Also we would be amazed if an animal could repeat a melody on first hearing – or after many hearings for that matter, and we would be willing to say of such an animal that he *knows* such-and-such a tune and that he is amazingly intelligent. But on the other hand the person's knowledge is not "scientific" – not explicit or systematic or related.

To get at the bottom of these questions, what is called for is an elaboration of what is meant by the word "know." We do not have any firm rule for distinguishing between knowledge that manifests itself only in action ("knowing how"), and theoretical or self-conscious knowledge ("knowing that"). In fact, a first step of pragmatic philosophy is to show that the real meaning of our theoretical knowledge must be found in some kind of a "knowing how" – even if it is a knowing how to think on a subject.

Theoretical knowledge, that is, knowledge in the highest form of which human beings are capable, has *two* features: (1) it involves a seeing of the causes, the interrelationships, the laws or principles which govern the understood phenomenon; (2) it also involves a firm, living, unswerving confidence in the fact known. It is interesting to observe that in some circumstances we may speak of a man "knowing" something, when only one of the above features is present. For example, a very primitive man may be said to "know" that the sun will rise tomorrow, although he may be quite ignorant of the physical laws involved in the movement of the celestial bodies. On the other hand, a man may make his living designing aircraft of various kinds, may have a quite thorough understanding of the principles behind flight, and yet have some kind of phobia against going up in a plane. He may have designed a plane, supervised its construction, seen it at the end to the runway and be willing to say, "I know it will fly," – and really know it too –, and yet not be willing to go up in it.

The pragmatists, particularly James and Dewey, have succeeded in shocking people by emphasizing the fact that knowledge manifests itself ordinarily in unhesitating action. Of course, that is one of the manifestations of true knowledge. But common sense protests that to know is not merely to have a great confidence, but it is primarily to understand, to see. Thus the readiness to act without hesitation is just plain foolishness unless this action turns out to be appropriate – that is, to reveal some prior conception of the principles governing the situation. (And the action can be *appropriate* and yet mistaken – i.e., there are some errors which are remarkably "reasonable" and seductive.) All of this is taken account of in Peirce's view of knowledge as abduction.

An organism thus can both be confident and respond appropriately (and successfully) – as a bird does in flying – but here we do not speak of knowledge in its very highest sense simply because all theoretical understanding is missing. If a pragmatist asks us for the "cash value" of this phrase "theoretical understanding" there is an answer at hand: a theoretical understanding permits an organism to respond appropriately under a much wider variety of conditions than the merely normal conditions. The instincts of animals are notoriously fixed and inflexible. The most trivial alteration of the environment from the normal pattern often serves to thwart the organism in an almost ludicrous way. The organism "knows" how to do something, but this knowledge is not theoretical. It is what Socrates called "right opinion." It is not "knowledge" in its fullest sense.

In a weak sense then we may say that the bird knows how to fly, or even that the stomach knows how to digest food, but the full sense of the word "know" involves the comprehension of a rule and is found (evidently) only in the higher animals.

Now of course, Peirce is an empiricist and he rejects the notion of innate ideas. But, in view of the continuity of nature and hence of man's mind with the structure of his own body and the world, he does hold that there is an innate *feel* for the truth, an innate tendency for the mind to hit upon good hypotheses. Technically, Peirce speaks of innate ideas, "but the innateness of an idea admits of degree, for it consists in the tendency of that idea to present itself to the mind." (6.416)

It is not surprising for Peirce that the human brain, adapted on every hand for the real world and the real laws of physics that govern that world – the laws of chemistry having to do with smell and taste, the laws of sound having to do with air in vibration, the laws of light relating to color and optics, the laws of biology having to do with the care and functioning of the human body – that a brain so adapted and so saturated through and through with the laws of physics and biology would, when it became ready to study the world scientifically or systematically, stumble with relative speed upon correct or nearly correct hypotheses. This is a phenomenon no less true of the esoteric parts of science than of the parts with which the mind might conceivably have more experience – it is, for example, no less true of researches in quantum mechanics than in studies in the early stages of mechanical physics. In these modern studies the investigators are led to try mathematical equations which seem somehow "fitting" or "beautiful" and in this way often come to important insights. But why some equations should seem "likely" or "beautiful" is just the mystery we are considering – a mystery compounded by nature's apparently finding them so too, or, if not beautiful, then useful or coherent. But if the mind is indeed "kin to" nature or "in tune" with nature, as Peirce claims, it is so in a very basic way indeed – in such a way that not only are our theories about the so-called "Newtonian" world surprisingly accurate, as indeed might be explained by the mind's acquaintance with macroscopic phenomena, but also the same holds true for the microscopic world, where the mind has no conscious opportunity for learning from ordinary experience. (Though here again, in the building up of the body a tremendous amount of information of the world of the atom and the molecule, and perhaps of sub-atomic physics too, is implicit.)

To be sure, Peirce's theory is quite vague – an objection which would have had no force with Peirce since vagueness is appropriate when dealing with matters on which we have little detailed information, which we seek to know only in broad outline. For Peirce a good theory is as vague and loose as possible, while yet explaining known phenomena. Such a broad theory is desirable because it is less likely to be ruined by small bits of new information. Peirce's theory of the mind's kinship with nature is a good theory indeed under this criterion.

If the theory is true, it has wide implications for the study of aesthetics, morality, and religion – areas as yet so little understood in a really scientific way, and perhaps, as some say, not even amenable to that approach, or only amenable to it in a highly modified form. The fact that Peirce's theory has wide implications also makes it a good theory, for it is all the easier to test and examine for this reason. Like all "idealistic" theories, it is fruitful of consequences and suggestions in a way more pedestrian or "materialistic" hypotheses are not. (cf. 5.599f.)

Peirce's theory is relevant to so many fields because it gives a new importance and grounding for beliefs or attitudes held by large numbers of men through the ages on *instinct*, or, if that is too technical a word or is thought to prejudice the issue, on simple feeling. The source of aesthetic pleasure, for example, is quite a mystery, but it is made far more mysterious by the amazing unanimity men show in their judgments of art. One of Peirce's most fundamental theses was that human reason is so weak that no individual ought to place overweening confidence in any truth he has discovered unless he can persuade all candid minds to agree with him (a thing most easily done in mathematics and accomplished only with great difficulty in most other fields). From this viewpoint the exceedingly short life span of most scientific theories contrasts amazingly with the agreement men share on ethical and artistic questions – fields alleged to be subjective beyond all hope. Whether Beethoven or Mozart were great artists who produced beautiful works is a perfectly settled question (though there might be debate as to how to rank them.) The same is true in painting and sculpture. That Greek sculpture and architecture was of very high quality is a judgment shared by virtually every living soul who has had the opportunity to know about these works. The time span is impressive – and another thousand years can be added by examining artifacts of various kinds found in Egyptian tombs – work that almost never fails to please the modern eye (and in this case the style has not been in a position to permeate civilized taste in the way that Greek works could, since many of the Egyptian works have been largely unknown or at least neglected through the intervening millenia).

Moral maxims can be shown to have displayed the same kind of perseverance of rough agreement in the most diverse ages and places.[4]

For Peirce it is entirely wrong to pretend that such deep-rooted feelings and sentiments are merely epiphenomena upon a blind play of dead atoms. To dismiss these phenomena this way is to approach the world with nominalistic eyes – and therefore to see nothing where there is everything important to be seen.

It would be an obvious criticism to charge that Peirce is urging us or encouraging us to believe in things – whether moral, metaphysical, or physical theories – merely because we have a very strong tendency to think them true. This over-simplifies what Peirce is saying. Peirce is saying indeed that in the case of a theory that exercises this rather occult attraction

---

[4] C. S. Lewis has collected a quite impressive list of moral maxims from diverse ages and places – impressive in that they are so similar to each other and to modern adages. See his *The Abolition of Man* (New York: The Macmillan Company, 1963), pp. 51ff. This point is certainly debatable. Perhaps one could collect a list of cynical maxims from all ages with equal case. La Rochefoucauld is a gold mine of them: he is the Devil's answer to Solomon. But then even the cynical maxims would probably be similar to each other, and that is all that is needed for the point at issue. Also it is interesting that cynical maxims are usually uttered with a semi-humorous intent, the humor depending upon our recognition that they go against our "higher nature."

over us we ought seriously to entertain it – examine it and test it, not, certainly, because it is going to come out true, but rather because it has a *high chance* of being true – a chance almost infinitely higher than in the case of a theory that does not pull us at all – some *ad hoc* theory which of course *might* be true, but which somehow seems silly or inappropriate to the investigator. Both what Peirce has affirmed and what he has not affirmed are important. He has not given a ridiculous theory that justifies whatever notion may please one, but he has shown that this very feeling of attraction is our indispensable guide and our only hope in the abductive process. But there is no excuse for not then going ahead and drawing out fully the consequences of a theory and subjecting them to a merciless series of tests, "insofar as possible."

On this point Russell agrees:

Every one who has done any kind of creative work has experienced, in a greater or less degree, the state of mind in which, after long labour, truth, or beauty, appears, or seems to appear, in a sudden glory – it may be only about some small matter, or it may be about the universe. The experience is, at the moment, very convincing; doubt may come later, but at the time there is utter certainty. I think most of the best creative work, in art, in science, in literature, and in philosophy, has been the result of such a moment. Whether it comes to others as to me, I cannot say. For my part, I have found that, when I wish to write a book on some subject, I must first soak myself in detail, until all the separate parts of the subject-matter are familiar; then, some day, if I am fortunate, I perceive the whole, with all its parts duly interrelated. After that, I only have to write down what I have seen. The nearest analogy is first walking all over a mountain in a mist, until every path and ridge and valley is separately familiar, and then, from a distance, seeing the mountain whole and clear in bright sunshine.

This experience, I believe, is necessary to good creative work, but it is not sufficient; indeed the subjective certainty that it brings with it may be fatally misleading. William James describes a man who got the experience from laughing-gas; whenever he was under its influence, he knew the secret of the universe, but when he came to, he had forgotten it. At last, with immense effort, he wrote down the secret before the vision had faded. When completely recovered, he rushed to see what he had written. It was: "A smell of petroleum prevails throughout." What seems like sudden insight may be misleading, and must be tested soberly when the divine intoxication has passed.[5]

So Peirce's theory does not mean, for example, that the morality of Western man is justified just because it is his and he likes it. Nor is Peirce suggesting that my aesthetic criteria are certain to be quite perfect because

[5] *A History of Western Philosophy* (New York: Simon and Schuster, 1945), pp. 123f.

they are mine and I like them. But he is suggesting that my moral and aesthetic criteria are *likely* to be on the right track, will probably *tend* to be correct – and this the more I widen my experience in those fields and submit myself to the training and education of those who already have long experience in these fields.

And here in embryo is surely the answer to those who, on the one hand, point to tribes in Africa or people on isolated South Sea islands, and point out moral or aesthetic preferences the most peculiar, in an effort to show how baseless and accidental are our own; and the answer to those, on the other hand, who want to hark back to some kind of primitive morality or aesthetic standard – perhaps taking as their ideal one of these same tribes.

The fault in going to the primitives or to isolated societies, whether for a positive or a negative purpose, lies in the very fact of their isolatedness. *We* are in a position to see *them* and judge and accept their criteria if we want, but *they* have not been in a position to see and accept *ours*. And the fact that most often primitivism is rejected by the great civilizations may just as well show that from the higher perspective and wider experience of the "high" civilizations, they sense the inferiority of the primitives as that they are prejudiced in favor of their own. And the fact that these minority groups tend to give up what is peculiar to their own standards when they have long been exposed to some major civilization, may indeed be used to indicate that in these matters, might makes right, but may also indicate that right makes might, that they recognize the overall superiority of the "civilized" ideals, over against, say, cannibalism. (I am speaking mostly in terms of general ethical *theory*, or of moral *ideals*. In practice, of course, "civilized" men who are adventurous enough to go to administer colonies may often be the moral inferiors of the natives.)

In the case of the Judeo-Christian ethic, with its supreme command of love of neighbor, it has grown from a small root and origin and has taken its hold on the minds of men all over the world, and I suppose the majority of moral analysts have concerned themselves rarely with improving it – the Utilitarians and others have tried with indifferent success – but rather with justifying it and grounding it. This at least is the way Peirce would incline to view these matters, and though the moral history of the world may not prove Peirce's point, it can be viewed from his perspective with as much or more ease than from others. And again it has the advantage of not leading to sceptical conclusions – conclusions which *no* man *can* live by and few want to.

An important by-product of Peirce's theory is the wonderful way it makes brothers out of the artists and scientists. Scientists have tended to look upon artists with a feeling compounded of wonder and contempt – contempt for the inexactness and utter subjectivity of the artist's work, but wonder and sometimes fear at his ability to play almost at will upon the heart-strings. And the artist looks upon the scientist as a man (if indeed he could bring himself to use or abuse the word thus) who has cut himself off from all that makes life rich or interesting – from all the deeper aspects of reality – not seeing of course that the best scientists are themselves nothing but artists, but having the aim, not merely of creating interesting and beautiful theories, but of discovering the interesting and beautiful plan laid down long ages ago by nature. The artist does not see the scientist's thrill when he has come to an idea that God himself had come to ages ago. The delights are of the same kind for both professions, and though one is more free than the other, both follow a process at bottom identical in the two cases. Peirce sums it up nicely: "The universe as an argument is necessarily a great work of art, a great poem." (5.119)

It is also worth nothing here what will have already have suggested itself to the reader – that Peirce's theory is conformable to religion in general, and in particular has much in common with the ancient Judeo-Christian doctrines that man was created in "God's image." Genesis, besides using that phrase, also says at one point that, quoting God, "Man has become like us, knowing good from evil." From the context, which has to do with moral knowledge, it is clear that an instinctive kind of knowledge is meant, since no code or list of commands is mentioned. And for the purpose of the philosophical points it is a matter of indifference with how much orthodoxy or literalness one looks at Genesis so long as the main points are understood, since, as it happens, Peirce and Genesis say much the same thing in the end, only Peirce elaborates the point and offers a suggestion as to how it came about. There is no evidence that Peirce ever thought about the Biblical doctrine of the *imago dei* in connection with his theory, but he would no doubt have delighted in finding his point already suggested in so venerable a document, particularly as it is so fundamental a point and was arrived at independently.

To object to all of this on the ground that it is a form of argument much too anthropomorphic, would again be no objection to Peirce. That it is anthropomorphic is, indeed, the whole point. Peirce accepts that form of argument, as being highly powerful in explanatory power and rejects competing theories on the ground that they are sterile.

I hear you say: "This smacks too much of an anthropomorphic conception." I reply that every scientific explanation of a natural phenomenon is a hypothesis that there is something in nature to which the human reason is analogous; and that it really is so all the successes of science in its applications to human convenience are witnesses. They proclaim that truth over the length and breadth of the modern world. In the light of the successes of science to my mind there is a degree of baseness in denying our birthright as children of God and in shamefacedly slinking away from anthropomorphic conceptions of the universe. (1.316)

There is a brilliantly suggestive essay written by the great French savant, Henri Poincaré, in which almost all of the points made by Peirce are raised independently, except the crucial hypothesis that the mind is in tune with nature. The essay is worth studying in its entirety, but for our purposes here we may quote some of the passages which are more striking:

... this feeling, this intuition of mathematical order, that makes us divine hidden harmonies and relations. . . . (p. 35)
    ... this delicate feeling so difficult to define. . . . (*Ibid.*)
A first hypothesis now presents itself: the subliminal self is in no way inferior to the conscious self; it is not purely automatic; it is capable of discernment; it has tact, delicacy; it knows how to choose, to divine. (p. 39)
    ... What is the cause that, among the thousand products of our unconscious activity, some are called to pass the threshold while others remain below? Is it a simple chance which confers this privilege? Evidently not ...
    It may not be surprising to see emotional sensibility invoked *a propos* of mathematical demonstrations which, it would seem can interest only the intellect. This would be to forget the feeling of mathematical beauty, of the harmony of numbers and forms, of geometric elegance. This is a true esthetic feeling that all real mathematicians know, and surely it belongs to emotional sensibility. (pp. 39f.)

It is clear from what Poincaré says in this essay that his greatest difficulty is in understanding how the subconscious mind is able to hit upon a good or plausible combination of ideas when the number of possible ones is unlimited. He is reduced to saying that the subconscious mind must somehow be able actually and really to go through a vast, incredible number of possible combinations (the number of which "frightens the imagination," p. 41). This is not entirely probable. Nor is Poincaré able to suggest any explanation for this amazing ability of the mind, even if it really does try out this countless multitude of ideas, to hit upon any good ones from the literally infinite number of possible combinations that must exist but cannot be brought into view because of their sheer quantity. One is almost driven to the conclusion that there is some kind of "divining" of likely combinations – even if the vast bulk of these are of no use.

[6] Henri Poincaré, "Mathematical Creation," in *The Creative Process*, Brewster Ghiselin, ed. (N.Y.: The New American Library, 1952), pp. 35ff. Poincaré's essay in its entirely is worth examining.

Poincaré really passes over the problem of recognizing good combinations once made. He says they have an appeal to our aesthetic sensibility and thus are allowed to break through to the conscious mind. This seems plausible, but says little by way of explanation for how the mind is able to test only reasonably plausible combinations out of the infinity at its disposal. Merely to say that useful combinations appeal to an aesthetic sensibility is to raise profound and difficult questions. Peirce's hypothesis offers a suggestion that points the way to a possible solution.

Peirce's theory of instinct and the mind's in-tune-ment with nature is a suggestion, like so many of Peirce's, in the best tradition of philosophy. It suggests a way of looking at the world; it answers, at least in a vague way, some of the persistent puzzles of modern thought; it opens the door to further thought and development. It shares these features with Descartes' *cogito* doctrine, with Hume's sceptical approach, with Kant's doctrine of categories of thought. Like those theories it is a great imaginative leap – and that apart from whether it is true or not.

In addition to that, the doctrine tends to close the gap between man and nature – in this sense it helps with the mind-body problem. It does not solve the problem of what is consciousness, to be sure, but it does bring the mind of man closer to nature, and allows it a certain "feel" for the unconscious world. Actually, in Peirce's thought the world is brought closer to the mind rather than *vice versa* in his doctrine of panpsychism, but the effect is the same either way – men need not feel so hopelessly estranged from nature that there is no chance of knowing her secrets and her laws, at least to an ever growing degree.

Finally, there is a striking confirmation of Peirce's theory in the writing of Hume – the man who perhaps more than any other embodied almost all of the opinions Peirce held to be false, a living catalogue of errors. The key passage occurs in Hume's *Treatise*.[7] Where he says with all possible emphasis that,

> . . . *all our reasonings concerning causes and effects are deriv'd from nothing but custom; and that belief is more properly an act of the sensitive, than of the cogitative part of our nature.*

In the Enquiry [8] he makes the same point, saying that our common sense beliefs are determined by nothing else than a "blind and powerful in-

---

[7] David Hume, *A Treatise of Human Nature,* L.A. Selby-Bigge, editor (Oxford: At the Clarendon Press, 1888), p. 183.
[8] David Hume, "An Enquiry Concerning Human Understanding," *The English Philosophers from Bacon to Mill,* Edwin A. Burtt, editor (New York: The Modern Library, 1939), p. 680.

stinct of nature." Hume certainly had more reason than anyone before him to recognize that belief in these matters was not an affair of purely rational considerations, that if one set one's mind to an effort to find logical objections to common sense there were many at hand and powerful. And it is interesting to observe how Hume's false approach to philosophy (as it would appear to Peirce) led him to much the same point that Peirce held, but without a supporting rationale. Of course, Hume thought that this necessity of relying upon our "sensitive nature" was all the more reason for being a sceptic. But how strange it is to deplore and mistrust that "blind and powerful instinct of nature" which brings us to believe so many things, when, without that instinct, we should hardly be able to know anything at all. We should hardly have to worry about learning the high truths of philosophy since we should not be in a position to know those elementary practical truths which enable us to survive to a philosophical age! And stranger yet, to know those practical truths which enable us to grow old and prosperous and then deny that those principles catch any part of the spectrum of truth. But, as Peirce pointed out, Hume was a man strong in his principles, and faithful in his idolatrous worship to the god Obstinancy!

This discussion is meant merely to give some rough indication of the direction which Peirce's theory of man's kinship with nature seems to lead us. Nature has been guiding man's mind and heart for countless generations, and in our searchings for truth, whether in physics, ethics, aesthetics, psychics, or whatever, we ignore our deep-rooted instincts at our own peril. Rather, our sentiments are nature's way of loading the dice in our favor in our search for truth. The mind is *inclined* toward the truth, and this is why hypothesis-making is frequently successful. Whether it is *slightly* inclined or *greatly* inclined is not so important as the fact that it is inclined *somewhat,* for whether slightly or greatly, the more we think and search the more this loading of the dice will tend to work in our favor. And in addition, this theory has the added merit – a merit according to Peirce's standards at least – of unifying the most diverse phenomena and having, if true, many varied consequences. Note again that the theory says nothing about the truth of any given insight suggested by instinct. In any given case such an insight is fallible. So on the one hand we have instinct, and on the other we have Peirce's empirical, "prope-positivist" side, the side dwelt upon by Buchler and others, the side concerned with the vital matter of testing and purifying such theories. Peirce's contribution to this side of the subject is recognized long since and established. But he was not lacking as a speculative philosopher.

C. THEORY AND PRACTICE

Peirce's view of human reason, tied as it is to a theory of instinct, has some extremely curious consequences, which are both interesting and profitable in themselves as well as shedding further light on the real meaning of his theory as it shows in its "practical" bearings its real significance. If indeed we are to look at the "upshot" of a concept or hypothesis to see its real meaning, we cannot neglect to do this with Peirce's theory of abduction itself, his theory of the theory-making process.

How Peirce views the connection between reason and instinct as the connection bears on human life and conduct is developed in three of the most stimulating and creative essays which Peirce wrote. The editors of the *Collected Papers,* following hints left by Peirce, have entitled these three essays, "Theory and Practice," "Practical Concerns and the Wisdom of Sentiment," and "Vitally Important Topics."

Perhaps the point of these essays can be summarized in the following excerpt:

In regard to the greatest affairs of life, the wise man follows his heart and does not trust his head. This should be the method of every man, no matter how powerful his intellect. More so still, perhaps, if mathematics is too difficult for him, that is to say, if he is unequal to any intricate reasoning whatsoever. Would not a man physically puny be a fool not to recognize it, and to allow an insane megalomania to induce him to enter a match game of football? But the slightest of physical frames might as well attempt to force back a locomotive engine, as for the mightiest of mental giants to try to regulate his life advantageously by a purely reasoned-out theory. (1.653)

Peirce supports this thesis with several interesting considerations. The first is that philosophy, in so far as it is a science, should be pursued by the scientific method. Now, the scientific method, in its highest form, looks, as he says, for the Truth of things, with no regard whatever to possible applications of these truths to human life and conduct. This is not, of course, to say that one should ignore practical applications as they may present themselves, nor is it to say that one cannot search for the solution to practical problems with the scientific method. But in doing these things one has departed that far from science's ideal, which is a completely disinterested pursuit of the way things are. Therefore, one ought not approach the study of philosophy with one eye always on the likely practical consequences of whatever theory may be under consideration. In the search for truth, whether in science or philosophy, it is always a very hard task to keep oneself objective, and this can hardly be done at all if one is forever nervous of the possible consequences of various points of view. *"All things"* are, or should be, pure theory to science. (5.589)

But it may reasonably be objected that possible practical consequences [9] are an integral part of any theory and neither can nor should be ignored. Peirce's position is that they should be ignored, when the theories in question bear on "vitally important matters," such as morality and religion, love and marriage, politics, and all similar matters. The ultimate reason Peirce has for taking what may appear to be so strange a position is that the reason of any one man, or even of one generation, is too weak and feeble a tool for a person to risk anything very important, in a personal sense, on what it happens to say at one moment. Though reason is weak, it is strong enough to be able to recognize how weak it is:

The very theory of reasoning, were we resolutely to attack it without any dread of mathematics, would furnish us conclusive reasons for limiting the applicability of reasoning to unimportant matters; so that, unless a problem is insignificant in importance compared with the aggregate of analogous problems, reasoning itself pronounces that there is a fallacy in submitting the question to reason at all. (1.652)

Were I willing to make a single exception to the principle I thus enunciate, and to admit that there was one study which was at once scientific and yet vitally important, I should make that exception in favor of logic; for the reason that if we fall into the error of believing that vitally important questions are to be decided by reasoning, the only hope of salvation lies in formal logic, which demonstrates in the clearest manner that reasoning itself testifies to its own ultimate subordination to sentiment. It is like a Pope who should declare *ex cathedra* and call upon all the faithful to implicitly believe on pain of damnation by the power of the keys that he was not the supreme authority. (1.672)

And again,

Reasoning is of three kinds. The first is necessary, but it only professes to give us information concerning the matter of our own hypotheses and distinctly declare that, if we want to know anything else, we must go elsewhere. The second depends upon probabilities. The only cases in which it pretends to be of value is where we have, like an insurance company, an endless multitude of insignificant risks. Wherever a vital interest is at stake, it clearly says, "Don't ask me." The third kind of reasoning tries what *il lume naturale*, which lit the footsteps of Galileo, can do. It is really an appeal to instinct. Thus reason, for all the frills it customarily wears, in vital crises, comes down upon its marrow-bones to beg the succour of instinct.

[9] This use of the word "practical" corresponds to the everyday use of the word as referring to "useful" to human interests, and is not to be confused with the more technical use of the word heretofore employed where is meant not only "useful" to human goals, but relevant to some possible experience.

Reason is of its very essence egotistical. In many matters it acts the fly on the wheel. Do not doubt that the bee thinks it has a good reason for making the end of its cell as it does. But I should be very much surprised to learn that its reason had solved that problem of isoperimetry that its instinct has solved. Men many times fancy that they act from reason when, in point of fact, the reasons they attribute to themselves are nothing but excuses which unconscious instinct invents to satisfy the teasing "whys" of the *ego*. The extent of this self-delusion is such as to render philosophical rationalism a farce.

Reason, then, appeals to sentiment in the last resort. Sentiment, on its side feels itself to be the man. That is my simple apology for philosophical sentimentalism. (1.630-632)

When no two metaphysicians agree, though they have used reason most rigorously in establishing their conclusions, how can a single individual hope to hit upon the truth by using his unaided reason? Socrates said that one ought not consult the "masses" on any important question – that when one needs a mundane task done, one goes to a specialist in the field, and, therefore, much more one should consult a specialist in vitally important matters. But this overlooks the fact that in any but the most mundane considerations there is no significant agreement among the "experts." Perhaps then the metaphysics of the masses, or of common sense, to put the case a bit more attractively, comes as close to the truth or perhaps closer than that of the various doctors of the subject. Santayana, who is even more of a common-sensist than Peirce, says, "I think that common sense, in a rough, dogged way, is *technically* sounder than the special schools of philosophy . . ." [10] Not just *practically,* but *technically.*

Does this mean that one ought to abandon the study of the higher subjects? By no means. It only means that one ought not alter one's life drastically at every alleged new discovery of reason.

It is far better to let philosophy follow perfectly untrammeled a scientific method, *predetermined* in advance of knowing to what it will lead. If that course be honestly and scrupulously carried out, the results reached, even if they be not altogether true, *even if they be grossly mistaken,* cannot but be highly serviceable for the ultimate discovery of truth. Meantime, sentiment can say, "Oh well, philosophical science has not by any means said its last word yet; and meantime I will continue to believe so and so." (1.644, my emph.)

The case may perhaps be illustrated by imagining a man who sets upon the study of ethics with a view in mind of radically reforming his life in

[10] *Op. cit.*, p. v.

accordance with whatever truth he may learn. Since the use of unaided reason upon this problem historically seems to give rise to conclusions highly diverse, we may imagine that, like many others, this individual comes to the clear and certain conviction that ethics lacks any foundation at all, and that all moral behavior is folly. Now, if he undertakes to live in accordance with this new insight, his lot is likely to be an unhappy one. He will probably be unhappy in prison, where society will quickly and rightly place him, if not for his wickedness exactly, then for his uncommon lack of good judgment, and his unhappiness will be compounded greatly if, one day, it occurs to him that he has made an elementary mistake in the line of reasoning which brought him to his extraordinary conclusion in the first place. This man we may call *unwise*:

Sentimentalism implies conservatism; and it is of the essence of conservation to refuse to push any practical principle to its extreme limits – including the principle of conservation itself. We do not say that sentiment is *never* to be influenced by reason, nor that under no circumstances would we advocate radical reforms. We only say that the man who would allow his religious life to be wounded by any sudden acceptance of a philosophy of religion or who would precipitately change his code of morals at the dictate of a philosophy of ethics – who would, let us say, hastily practice incest – is a man whom we should consider *unwise*. The regnant system of sexual rules is an instinctive or sentimental induction summarizing the experience of all our race. That it is abstractly and absolutely infallible we do not pretend; but that it is practically infallible for the individual – which is the only clear sense the word "infallibility" will bear – in that he ought to obey it and not his individual reason, *that* we do maintain. (1.633)

Animals which we may presume know very little theory on any subject whatever, very seldom fall into *vitally* serious errors. By instinct they know enough of animal psychology to find a mate and raise offspring usually without engaging in maniacal and suicidal wars against animals of their own species. They know enough of applied physics and biology adequately to feed, shelter and defend themselves.

Certain qualifications and explanations must be made if this doctrine is to seem anything less than utterly irrational. First, one may point out that most men have practiced what Peirce is here preaching. Hume did not pretend to live by his theoretical discoveries, and would have thought mad anyone who did. It is not at all uncommon for great philosophers to hold moral theories which from the viewpoint of common sense can only be called monstrous, and at the same time live lives of the greatest charity and gentleness toward their fellow creatures. Nor would it strike anyone as unbelievable for a doctor of ethics who preached a very vigorous code

of morality to abscond with a large sum of money. Metaphysicians with
the most diverse views of time, some holding that it is an illusion, all look
at their watches. So common are events like these that one hardly notices
the wide gulf that separates theory and practice – and what reasons, if
any, lie behind the existence of that gulf.

Secondly, Peirce says, "vitally important matters" are, of all matters,
the "veriest trifles." Here we must be careful not to misunderstand him.
"Vitally important matters" are for Peirce *personal* in an extreme degree;
they do not concern the world of universal forms and truths. Too much
concern with these practical matters leads to *barbarism* (1.674), or to the
successful businessman mentality (at its worst, is meant, of course).

... suppose you embrace ... a conservative sentimentalism, modestly rate
your own reasoning powers at the very mediocre price they would fetch if
put up at auction, and then what do you come to? Why, *then,* the very first
command that is laid upon you, your quite highest business and duty, becomes, as everybody knows, to recognize a higher business than your business,
not merely an avocation after the daily task of your vocation is performed,
but a generalized conception of duty which completes your personality by
melting it into the neighboring parts of the universal cosmos. If this sounds
unintelligible, just take for comparison the first good mother of a family that
meets your eye, and ask whether she is not a sentimentalist, whether you
would wish her to be otherwise, and lastly whether you can find a better
formula in which to outline the universal features of her portrait than that
I have just given. I dare say you can improve upon that; but you will find
one element of it is correct – especially if your understanding is aided by
the logic of relatives – and that is that the supreme commandment of the
Buddhisto-christian religion is, to generalize, to complete the whole system
even until continuity results and the distinct individuals weld together. Thus
it is, that while reasoning and the science of reasoning strenuously proclaim
the subordination of reasoning to sentiment, the very supreme commandment of sentiment is that man should generalize, or what the logic of relatives
shows to be the same thing, should become welded into the universal continuum, which is what true reasoning consists in. But this does not reinstate
reasoning, for this generalization should come about, not merely in man's
cognitions, which are but the superficial film of his being, but objectively in
the deepest emotional springs of his life. In fulfilling this command, man
prepares himself for transmutation into a new form of life, the joyful Nirvana in which the discontinuities of his life shall have all but disappeared.
(1.673)

Rational considerations are thus said to have bearing upon our vitally
important concerns, but not in a hasty or rash fashion. Instinct may be
improved and taught, but only slowly and over a period of time, after
long acquaintance with theory:

Instinct is capable of development and growth – though by a movement which is slow in the proportion in which it is vital; and this development takes place upon lines which are altogether parallel to those of reasoning. . . . The soul's deeper parts can only be reached through its surface. In this way the eternal forms, that mathematics and philosophy and the other sciences make us acquainted with, will by slow percolation gradually reach the very core of one's being; and will come to influence our lives; and this they will do, not because they involve truths of merely vital importance, but because they are ideal and eternal verities. (1.648)

In this way we are to understand the point regarding the fact that animals do not fall into vital errors. If we were content to live as animals do we should give up the sciences altogether. This is not what is recommended at all. In fact, Peirce wants everyone to become imbued with the scientific spirit – to lose his individuality in the search for the most general truths. But while we are in our present state of ignorance we must understand the difference between scientific hypotheses – whether they concern chemistry or ethics – hypotheses which may have enough merit to justify long and expensive investigation, but which it would be unwise to act upon forthwith, and the instincts by which we judge on the vitally important affairs. In one's personal life, failing positive discoveries in the fields of morality, metaphysics, and religion, one must maintain a modest conservatism, and the highest possible respect for *experience*:

If, walking in a garden on a dark night, you were suddenly to hear the voice of your sister crying to you to rescue her from a villain, would you stop to reason out the metaphysical question of whether it were possible for one mind to cause material waves of sound and for another mind to perceive them? If you did, the problem might probably occupy the remainder of your days. In the same way, if a man undergoes any religious experience and hears the call of his Saviour, for him to halt till he has adjusted a philosophical difficulty would seem to be an analogous sort of thing, whether you call it stupid or whether you call it disgusting. If on the other hand, a man has had no religious experience, then any religion not an affectation is as yet impossible for him; and the only worthy course is to wait quietly till such experience comes. No amount of speculation can take the place of experience. (1.655)

Peirce further says that true science cannot succeed if it is oriented toward practical interests. The medical researcher, who does all his work with an eye on finding cures for human ills is ruined as a scientific man, though "he may do a great deal for human life." (1.619)

What are we to say of this? First, it is debatable whether "pure" science should have precedence over "practical" science, though the mere suggestion would be heresy to Peirce. One might be tempted to say that "pure" research might ultimately lead to even more practical results than efforts frankly practical in nature. On the other hand, it is perhaps equally plausible to argue that as many "pure theoretical" discoveries are made in the pursuit of "practical" ends as would be made in direct pursuit of them, and this is plausible because it appears that any number of the most important of all scientific discoveries have been hit upon by accident, by men working (as often as not) on some practical problem. By this I mean to suggest that many of the most important new discoveries necessarily lie in unsuspected directions, and consequently may be hit upon nearly as well by accident as any other way, and meanwhile practical interests give a motive force to keep a small army of investigators at work in varied fields. Of course, science can never advance if these profoundly suggestive discoveries are not followed up by the theoreticians, if they are merely ignored and left to the side by the men concerned with some specific practical problem – but it might be a matter of doubt if there are many scientists of no matter how humble rank who will not greet wih excitement any radically new phenomenon they may run into by accident. On the other hand, it is easy to defend Peirce on this point. For no matter how many important theoretical discoveries may be hit upon in the course of efforts to establish man in space, for example, it seems also probable that that much effort devoted to more basic enquiries would be more productive of basic discoveries. Consider the mysteries connected with biological processes, or the brain, or parapsychology! But there is no practical way to get men as interested in putting all that money into these fields. The money being spent on space research, if not spent there, would probably not be spent at all.

* * *

Like the music of Mozart, which has the most profound ambiguity – a tension between the highest joy and the deepest melancholy, Peirce's work weaves into a complex fabric the most diverse themes. This intricate interconnectedness is perhaps as well illustrated by the above quoted passages and discussion as anywhere – and as well illustrated by this whole essay of Peirce's as by any of the others. This whole essay is the work of the greatest possible genius. Without passing judgment as to whether it is exactly true or not, there is no denying is suggestiveness. It is misleading perhaps to imagine that the subject of this essay is confined to "theory and practice." It could as appropriately be considered as a discussion of the relation between science and religion, or philosophy and life, or "logic and mysticism," or "reason and instinct." A detailed comparison of Peirce's thoughts on this subject with Bertrand Russell's book, *Logic and Mysticism,* would no doubt be rewarding in the extreme, and the same is true of Bergson's doctrine of the artificiality and misleading nature of reason as compared to instinct's sure feel for the truth. And again the same subject is discussed by Santayana in his book on the relation between reason and "animal faith," and the results of Santayana's work are similar to Peirce's. When so many men of differing approaches have such a basic point in common, we certainly have justification for taking that point with the utmost seriousness.

CHAPTER V

THE CARTESIAN CIRCLE:
A FINAL LOOK AT SCEPTICISM

The so-called Cartesian Circle problem is scepticism in its most difficult form. We hope in this final section to examine this problem in the light of Peirce's epistemological principles. This ought to be helpful both from the standpoint of perhaps "answering" the problem, as well as from the standpoint of clarifying Peirce's doctrines by application of them, to yet another philosophical difficulty.

It was Descartes who brought to the attention of the philosophical world the following problem, wonderful both in its simplicity and its difficulty. What reasons, he asked in effect, do we have for trusting our power of reasoning? How do we know that what seem to us the most cogent and powerful arguments are not merely strong illusions? Even on the surface this is an important and difficult question, but a little reflection reveals a truly profound and hopeless complication: all thinking which we may do on this problem *presupposes* the reliability of our reasoning power, which itself is just what is in question. Thus to answer the question it seems necessary to think, but the possibility of thinking validly is just the question.

Descartes himself slurs over the problem. In fact, from the viewpoint of his own principles we may say that he ignores the problem altogether. On the other hand, from a certain viewpoint and interpreted correctly, we shall finally have to admit that even Descartes succeeded in giving the only appropriate answer possible to this problem. That is, he says that what we see clearly and distinctly we must, perforce, accept as true. But how we understand this doctrine is crucial.

We have already seen that for Hume there are sharp lines of distinction between what is known, what is probable, and what is believed by custom or habit. To know something "certainly" and to know it "probably" are, for Hume, two quite different kinds of knowing, of utterly "disagreeing natures." And we have seen that for Hume no man may be said to "know" anything, since Hume means by "know" a perfect, infallible, indubitable certainty. In particular, deductive reason, which pretends to give us precisely these kinds of certainties, lacks infallible axioms (without which all that follows is vitiated), and moreover it has no sure means of avoiding errors as the deductive process unfolds.

Even more obviously "matters of fact" are dubitable, depending as they all do upon sense experience or memory.

We *really* believe things, according to Hume, only because of custom and habit. But these of course have not even a pretence of being reasonable. They are simple animal propensities, nothing more. They merely overpower us.

Now some modern pragmatists have urged that really all we mean by "to know" is "to have a very strong expectation of." This is no doubt an oversimplification, but we need not deny that this is one of the overt manifestations of knowing. It is apparent that Hume was much in sympathy with this view, for he says,

Without the influence of custom, we should be entirely *ignorant* of every matter of fact beyond what is immediately present to the memory and senses. We should never know how to adjust means to ends, or to employ our natural powers in the production of any effect. (*Enquiry,* V, 1; my emphasis)

If we take this language literally the results are very interesting; we may be said to have our *ignorance* dispelled and to gain *knowledge* through the power of habit and custom. According to this view, the formation of a habit would actually be a species (for Hume the only species) of *reason*. Custom yields knowledge, which in turn is a set of expectations. The repeated experience of something (the ringing of a bell at meal time, the rising of the sun, etc.) gives rise in us, by virtue of protoplasm's habit-taking nature, to a custom. We call this the law of association. In slightly different contexts we also call it induction. And we say that it teaches us things and we know them. So, at least, goes Hume.

The above is the usual line of argument employed by sceptics. We present it only because of its relative completeness and plausibility. What we wish to accomplish here, however, is to show what reasons there are, given Peirce's view of reason, for trusting reason. Of course, when we speak of Peirce's view of reason we mean abduction and its related concepts.

We have already gone a long way toward answering the sceptic in our previous accounts of abduction. Abduction, we recall, is insight. It is seeing things harmoniously, coherently, generally, economically. It is the mind's effort to render matters which surprise into matters of course. It is a manifestation of an organism's general dislike of surprises, except in play, where they stimulate. Abduction is the path of least resistance in thought. A fallacy, understood not merely as a mistake in reasoning, but rather as a tempting, seductive mistake, comes from the mind's tendency to take the path of least resistance *prematurely* – i.e., leaving out significant data and rushing to an inviting conclusion. Fallacies, understood in this way, shed important light upon valid reasoning processes, which are shown to be matters of harmonious insight into a problematic or disconnected situation. This "insight" consists in seeing the various strands of causal interconnection involved in the situation, or in grasping the law or principle of operation of the phenomenon. This is how the mind works. This is what reason is.

On this view of reason, *philosophy* may be understood as the effort of the human mind to detect the overall patterns presented to us by experience. There is no way to prove (deductively) that any "insight" into the nature of things is the correct one. In matters of the physical sciences (as contrasted to philosophy) the situation is fortunate for although we may not be able to prove a theory, we can at least make an effort to falsify it. (Although this is a much weakened form of the now defunct verification position, it is not without grave difficulties of its own; yet it is a helpful notion and roughly corresponds at least to what scientists do). In matters of music, art, literature, as well as of metaphysics, ethics, politics, economics, and religion, affairs are not so fortunate, for it is difficult conclusively to falsify any given alleged insight. All that can be done, usually, is to get people, by appropriate means, to see the awkwardness, inappropriateness, or, on the other hand, the naturalness or fittingness of a position. We have seen that John Wisdom, in his famous essay, "Gods," shows that when all the facts are known there may still remain a question of fact. That is, the bare facts may need an interpretation. There is, as he says, a "logic of interpretation." This, of course, is what abduction or "insight" is all about. Men before Newton knew that apples fell, that the tides came in and out, that the moon revolved around the earth. But Newton saw a pattern where others had not. This is the essence of scientific discovery – or the essence of metaphysical discovery for all that. Thus both science and art are matters of seeing patterns. There is no "proof" in either case, except that in science there is in most cases some degree of disproof available if the theory is false. Bad science, like bad art, over-simplifies.

An hypothesis, then, is the seeing of some pattern. Induction is based on an hypothesis, which, in turn, is based on a pattern seen, or thought to be seen, in experience. That nature is uniform is an *hypothesis* – a sheer leap of insight, a guess. It is not "proved" by experience – not in the least. Of course, it is not disproved by experience, but even this is not the ground of its acceptance. Many related theories might not be disproved by experience. It is "proved" by its overwhelming naturalness, its fittingness, its appeal to all of our sensibilities. Mathematical, or other "proofs" of the validity of induction, particularly when dealing with a source of phenomena which may be infinite, are all bogus, as can always be demonstrated conclusively, because it is just a logical fact that a radical change in nature, or for that matter the end of nature altogether, is possible.

The appeal of certain insights to our sense of harmony may, according to Peirce, be a sign of the communion of our spirits with God. We cannot penetrate into the nature of matter as such. Matter is for us a dead surd. All we see, or can see, are the laws, regularities, rationalities which matter embodies.[1] It is a call of Mind to mind. But we digress from speculation to Speculation.

Sherlock Holmes speaks of "reasoning backwards," meaning the process of hypothesis-building. "Reasoning backwards," or abduction, is, from the standpoint of formal logic, the fallacy of affirming the consequent. One reasons, "A is the case. But if B were the case too, then A would be a matter of course. Therefore, B may be the case." The logicians call this a fallacy, not because it is not a good way to reason about matters of fact – indeed it is not only a good way, it is the only way to reason about such matters – but only because, technically speaking, it is not infallible. But this is no news: we have always known that existential reasoning was liable to error. Scientific theories are often in error. But is not deductive reasoning also a matter of getting insights into the interrelations that exist among ideas, and are not these insights notoriously liable to error (as in geometry, for example)? True enough, for many types of proposed mathematical theorems a complete test is possible (such as are not possible in even the most rigorous physical sciences). But failing the discovery of such complete tests the theorem is said to be unproved and remains open to doubt in the same way hypotheses concerning nature are open. And it is also true that what was once thought to be a complete test may turn out to have involved some kind of unsuspected, hidden error.

[1] Compare Peirce: "... those characters of the real must be of the nature of thoughts or sufficiently so to impart some sense to our talking of thoughts conforming to those characters ... this thought or quasi-thought in which the characters of the real consist ..." Microfilm MSS. item 315, p. 30.

The process of reason is not essentially different in deduction or induction: it is always characterized by a looking for patterns. The differences have to do only with the possibility or ease or degree with which we may verify or falsify our hypotheses, which is to say, eliminate the possibility of other hypotheses.

The moral to all of this is that the idea of "proof" is tricky. Proof is essentially the appeal to animal propensities. A true or good theory warms our hearts, to use a high metaphor. It strikes us as fitting and irresistably attractive. This is why, philosophy aside, we believe in, know that the outside world exists. This theory of the existence of the outside world can not be verified, any more than some alternatives to it such as solipsism, nor is there a way in principle in which it might be falsified. We just know it is true. We have an insight into the true case. Nothing is proved merely by the fact that experience has not yet refuted it.

On Peirce's theory of knowledge, we have to ask what reason there is for trusting the "insights" we may get. Now do we know that these insights tend to lead us to the truth? Aside from simple pragmatic success, Peirce says that it is because these insights to which we come are arrived at by virtue of certain animal propensities, certain tendencies which our minds feel to view nature in a certain way. Our minds themselves are a part of nature and were formed under the guidance of nature's hand, and so may be assumed to be somehow "in tune with nature," in harmony with nature. Science gives us reason to believe something like this to have been the case. But why indeed are we inclined to believe the scientist? Only because the things he says generally point us to harmonious, inclusive, economical, unified ways of viewing phenomena. But our reasoning now has taken us in a circle. We trust our reasoning power because we trust our minds. But we trust our minds because we trust what the scientists tell us about the origin of our minds. And we trust what the scientists tell us because it is generally satisfying to our reason. But how can such plainly circular reasoning be justified? Perhaps it is because this is no ordinary circle. Perhaps it is because it is a circle which gathers up into itself all the important and fundamental things we believe; it does not leave anything out and it is eminently satisfying. Perhaps that is its only justification. Perhaps indeed that is what justification is!

The circularity involved in Peirce's way of looking at the matter differs only by its generality from the generally recognized problem of induction. We trust scientific induction because we believe nature is uniform. But this premise is itself only the result of a great induction. So induction is supported by induction.

But both of these problems are only sub-problems under the most general philosophic problem of all, the problem of the justification of reason. So far in this discussion we have been reasoning about reason. We have been trying to gain some insight into the phenomenon of gaining insights in general. Observe very carefully: *the whole enterprise is circular* – not just the particular arguments we have presented, but the whole enterprise.

As we indicated at the beginning, the problem that has revealed itself here goes back to Descartes' famous doubt. Among all the things he doubts is reason. Descartes failed to see the seriousness of this particular step because he proceeded without any further ado, to *reason* – first to his own existence, then to the existence of God, and so on. Grant, if you wish, that his proofs of his own existence and God's are ever so cogent and reasonable. What do they prove if the faculty of reason itself is still left in question? If God exists we may perhaps assume that his benevolence is such that he would not make our reasoning faculty systematically misleading. But the crucial, hopeless aspect of the problem is that if our reasoning power cannot be trusted, all remedies fail. We cannot even get to our own existence, much less God's. The sheerest scepticism results. If our reasoning power cannot be trusted, then our inquiries into the phenomenon of reasoning or any phenomenon whatever cannot be expected to do us any good or advance us one step out of scepticism. If the problem is drastic, we may expect the solution to be no less drastic.

A. THE THEORY OF TYPES AS APPLIED TO ORDINARY LANGUAGE

We hope to show that the so-called Theory of Types is a problem very analogous to the "Cartesian Circle" problem. And further we believe that when one understands the mistake involved in the Theory of Types he is well on his way toward a solution of the larger, analogous problem.

The Theory of Types has had an interesting history. It was proposed by Russell as a means of avoiding certain contradictions in Set Theory. There has been almost a conspiracy of silence concerning the blatantly *ad hoc* character of this ploy, as well as concerning its non-logical character – which is important relative to any claim to have reduced mathematical notions to *purely* logical ones.[2] And these criticisms apply equally to all the proposed modifications of Russell's original proposal.

Here, however, we are not particularly concerned with Set Theory,

[2] See S. Körner's *The Philosophy of Mathematics* (London, Hutchinson and Co., 1960). pp. 52ff.

mann that some restriction must be placed on ordinary language corresponding in function to the limitation the Theory of Types places on Set Theory.

Russell, in the introduction to *Principia Mathematica* says,

The imaginary sceptic, who asserts that he knows nothing, and is refuted by being asked if he knows that he knows nothing, has asserted nonsense, and has been fallaciously refuted by an argument which involves a vicious-circle fallacy. In order that the sceptic's assertion may become significant, it is necessary to place some limitation upon the things of which he is asserting his ignorance, because the things of which it is possible to be ignorant form an illegitimate totality.[3]

Waismann raises a similar point: "Take the case of the Liar, that is of the man who says, 'I am lying'; if he is lying he is speaking the truth, and if he is speaking the truth he is lying. We may interpret his statement as saying, 'All propositions which I assert are false.' "[4] Pointing out the "paradox" in such statements, Waismann makes this significant observation: "The decisive point to realize is that the phrase 'all propositions' is an illegitimate totality."[5]

The point we wish to make is simply that it is not true to say that "the phrase 'all propositions' is an illegitimate totality." Not only is such a statement not true, it will not even do as a statement of *policy*, even if one were to admit it to be an arbitrarily imposed policy. It is not a *possible* policy.

In the first place, the offending sentence is not true because there are countless occasions on which one might wish to refer to "all propositions" or use that phrase as the subject of a sentence, on which occasions the phrase not only would make perfect sense but also would be indispensible for the expression of the thought. This is a very important consideration, for if we oblige ourselves to avoid in every case propositions having for their subject the phrase "all propositions," we shall be prevented from saying many very sensible, very useful, and very true things. True or false, one would want to be able to say such things as, "All propositions may be written," "All propositions contain a subject," "All propositions contain the word 'all'," etc.

Waismann and Russell seem to think there must be something perni-
but rather with the assumption made by both Russell and Friedrich Wais-

---

[3] Volume I, Introduction.
[4] Friedrich Waismann, "Language Strata," *Logic and Language*, Antony Flew (editor), (New York: Doubleday and Co., 1965), p. 233.
[5] *Ibid.*

cious about a manner of speaking which even *permits* self-contradictory statements; whereas the truth may very well be that there is something pernicious (or impossible) about a manner of speaking which cannot express such.

But much more important than the fact that such a policy as Russell and Waismann suggest would preclude our saying many true and/or meaningful statements – much more important than that is the simple fact that if what Waismann asserts were true, then *he couldn't say it*. This constitutes right strong evidence against his position. For what the Theory of Types asserts essentially (as applied now to common language) is that "all propositions must be arranged in strata in such a way that one never encounters the unqualified subject 'all propositions.' " In that case, of course, the very policy statement is forbidden.

If one says, "One may never speak of 'all propositions,' " he has violated his policy in uttering it. (Of what is one forbidden even to *speak*? – Ah, but you must not speak of it in answering!)

Or again, if one says that all propositions must be arranged in strata in such a way that one never encounters the unqualified phrase "all propositions," then one must ask in what stratum one proposes to place that rule.

Evidently we have to be able to think of the totality of all propositions in order to carry on speculations such as these and in order to understand the Theory of Types, and we have to speak of this "forbidden totally" in forbidding to speak of it. The Theory of Types involves thus a self-contradiction (not simply a "paradox" – a weasel word). We have already seen that many propositions which speak of "all propositions" are not self-contradictory (including, for example, this one).

If it is permissible and even inevitable that one speak sometimes of "all propositions" – as those who enunciate the Theory of Types as here applied do – then there seems to be no point in arranging all propositions into strata, with the strange infinite regress that such a policy entails.

What all of this boils down to is that among all the kinds of propositions which we utter some of them are *self-reflexive*. Some propositions refer to themselves. (E.g., "This sentence is written here in black ink.") Among the many different self-reflexive sentences which one might imagine, some of them refer not only to themselves but also to all sentences whatever. (E.g., "All propositions are written in black ink.") Whether they are true or false is not relevant. What is relevant is their *meaning,* and in particular in the case of these latter kinds of sentences, whether or not their meaning is *self-consistent*. For among those self-reflexive sentences which refer to all sentences, *some* of them are self-contradictory, and some are not. There is nothing occult about this situation.

Let us consider some examples:

1) "All propositions are written in black ink." This sentence is self-reflexive and false. If it happens not to be written in black ink, it would be an example of the kind of thing that causes it to be false, but it is not self-contradictory. That is, its meaning is self-consistent. One could not tell from listening to it and examining the idea it expresses that it is false. One would have to consult experience.

2) "All propositions contain the word 'all.'" This sentence is similar to the above example. Its falsity cannot be determined by reference to itself as an example.

3) "All propositions are false." This is the interesting case referred to by Russell and Waismann. It is a simple self-contradiction and amounts to saying nothing whatever. It is not "paradoxical," i.e., a *seeming* contradiction; it is a real one. All propositions implicitly assume their own truth, and any proposition which then overtly denies its own truth has simply negated itself.

4) "All propositions are true." This is a false sentence, but as in (2) above, its falsity cannot be determined by an examination of its meaning alone. Hence, it is not *self*-contradictory. (The Hegelians might claim it is a true sentence!)

One could continue along this line to make up interesting and curious examples, but I know of none which will not lend itself to a straightforward analysis along the lines already presented. One need only understand the concepts of "self-reference" and "contradiction."

Once again, Russell and Waismann suffer under the apprehension that a language which *permits* self-contradiction must be flawed. This is the merest prejudice carried over, one supposes, from their experience with *closed* logical systems, the very point of which is to have a language calculus such that, the rules being followed, no self-contradiction is *possible*. What this discussion suggests is rather that such a closed system is impossible. And this is precisely what we should expect upon an epistemological view which is *organic*.

It may be that we have been grievously mislead by our apparent ability to construct closed systems, whether mathematical, logical, geometrical, or even philosophical. It may be that all such closed systems are essentially arbitrary, not succeeding in catching in a net logic, mathematics, or life as they are really lived and performed every day by everyone. Not, of course, that they are useless, nor that no one of them is not to be preferred for certain purposes to the others.

On this point we may recall Whitehead's remark that "... every finite set of premises must indicate notions which are excluded from its direct purview." [6] This is exactly the point made by that most remarkable discovery of Kurt Goedel. Goedel's Proof shows that it is impossible to demonstrate the internal consistency of most mathematical systems, including even such simple systems as that represented by the ordinary arithmetic of ordinal numbers. The proof shows that it will never be possible to know that a self-contradiction will not arise in such systems. The proof also demonstrates that arithmetic, for example, cannot be axiomatized, since it is always possible to generate an infinite number of true arithmetic statements which cannot be derived from one's given axioms. This means, in effect, that *each* true arithmetic statement can be considered an axiom. Nagel and Newman go so far as to generalize from Goedel's Proof to the following observation concerning the powers of the human mind: "[Goedel's Proof] does mean that the resources of the human intellect have not been, and cannot be, fully formalized, and that new principles of demonstration forever await invention and discovery." [7]

B. BELIEVING IS SEEING

The problem with the Theory of Types, as I suggested above, is not so much its (faulty) analysis of the problem with which it deals, as it is the fact that that problem itself is not the truly major problem. The real perplexity is not so much that sceptical propositions seem to have strange implications for themselves, as do some other general propositions; rather the truly general problem concerns the "Cartesian circle," i.e., the initial doubt of the reasoning faculty itself. This latter problem is not just a problem about what certain propositions mean or how they work, but is a problem about thinking itself. Russell evidently believes that the Theory of Types somehow serves to answer the Cartesian circle problem. At least he says that one cannot doubt all propositions because the latter is an "illegitimate totality." But whether the above analysis of the Theory of Types is right or wrong I believe it will become evident below that the Theory of Types is not coextensive with the problem of the Cartesian circle; rather, this latter problem is more general and more difficult.

Let us now ask and face this question: Is it reasonable to believe in reason? Let us translate this question into a form consonant with the

[6] Whitehead, *op. cit.*, pp. 2, 4.
[7] Ernest Nagel and James R. Newman, "Goedel's Proof" in *The World of Mathematics*, James R. Newman (ed.), (New York: Simon and Schuster, 1956), Vol. III, p. 1695. See also S. Körner, *op. cit.* pp. 91-97.

analysis of reason presented above. Reason was there said to be the faculty we have for grasping patterns in experience – moreover, not merely *any* patterns, but natural, fitting, illuminating patterns. Thus our question above is translated: Does a good pattern emerge to believe that good patterns catch the truth? Now philosophers have different answers to this question. For example, Hume thought he saw the radically untrustworthy character of our reasoning power. Thus, when thinking about thinking, Hume saw no good pattern. Yet, on the other hand, Peirce saw a very interesting pattern (i.e., roughly the circular argument described above). Now we must be clear that we are not looking for a logico-deductive proof – we are looking for a *reasonable* position. We are looking for a view that fits the known facts and is plausible and relevant. In all such matters the notion of "proof" is out of bounds – rather it is a matter of artistic insight: but No!: proof is always a kind of artistic insight.

Let us now suppose that Peirce is right: that reason is essentially an animal propensity to come into harmony with the truth. All falls into place nicely. But suppose we do not allow this. Suppose we doubt that reason will take us to the truth. What then? We are *paralyzed*. There is no move possible from this position. Any talk you make presupposes that talk can do some good, when that is the very thing in question.

But now let us at least admit that what our reason does is to *try* to see good patterns – regardless of whether it succeeds. This need not be a conclusion of *reason:* we actually *feel* this desire for harmony and this repugnance at chaos. We have a simple animal propensity to try to get patterns: that is to say we *do it* and *will do it*. (Cf. "Nature overcomes all doubts.") But *doing it,* we see a good pattern in the pattern-getting process, and are warmed – i.e., our reason is satisfied. So, since we do it, we see that it is reasonable to do it. Since we *do* reason, one result of this is that we see that reason is reasonable. But, you say, *suppose* reason leads to wrong results. What then? We answer: *we reason anyway:* our cells make us reason. But reasoning, we then see why it should lead to right results, and therefore we cannot believe your proposed supposition – it is not reasonable!

Someone objects: Are you saying that it is *impossible* effectively to doubt reason? Yes, it is impossible. We can form the words, but we cannot do the thing. We may kill ourselves, but we reason and trust our reasons as long as we live. One reasons while *sensing* even (since this also is a pattern getting process).

Now when we think about the situation we may see that we have merely grasped onto a presupposition, taken hold of an axiom or postulate when we take the first step of reason. That is to say that the first step of reason necessarily presupposes reason's probable or possible validity. But upon thinking about this axiom, this presupposition, we see clearly that it is rational and based upon good reasons. Reason leaps in, and sees that, though it had to leap (grasp onto an axiom), the leap was justified, but only in retrospect. Of course, reason really does not leap in: nature pushes it.

But again observe: a *good* leap *is* a proof. Any proof is a coming to see some data from a new and satisfying perspective. All proofs have the form of an embrace. *Believing is seeing!* This is a universal law, and not merely a peculiarity of the Cartesian circle problem (or the problem of God's existence – since many have claimed that belief in Him must preceed knowledge of Him).

To put the matter in other words: When we think, this activity presupposes that thinking will lead to the truth. Since we *will* think, we are logically compelled to believe that it will take us to the truth. We must believe thinking is reasonable if we think. So we may say: "I think: therefore I believe in reason." Here is a doctrine vastly more true and more important than Descartes'. This doctrine I claim is quite air-tight logically and has truly far-reaching results.

But upon our analysis (or rather Peirce's) it is tempting to believe that the sceptic may content himself with saying *not* that all reason is futile or false, but only "I think, therefore I must think and thinking pleases me." This seems a modest enough proposal. But of course it overlooks the ever-ready retort: "How do you know *that*?" The answer can only be, "By reasoning." (Note the use of the word "therefore.") That proposal, modest as it seemed to be, yet purported to be the announcement of a *truth*. So the presupposition that we were announcing at least one truth was still there, even in the alleged discovery that we were not approaching truths, or at least that there is no proof that we are. The serious making of any proposition presupposes the validity of the thinking process. The strong sceptical proposal (that there is no knowledge), if true, would be a truth, which shows the proposal itself is not true. In short, the denial of reason is a positive self-contradiction and quite unthinkable. It is not a matter of language strata. The weak sceptical proposal (above) still implicitly announces a truth, and thus belies its apparent modesty.

Even the perception of a feeling involves, as we saw in the early sections of this book, the interpretive, synthesizing, organizing – which is to say – *reasoning* powers of the mind. So the declaration that one presently feels something would not be truth enunciated independently of reliance upon reason.

These objections do not apply to the proposition, "I think, therefore I believe in reason." If one asks how one gets that truth, the answer is at hand. "By reason, which I have announced I trust. I believe in reason by reason." *There is no self-contradiction here. There is only circularity.* Here then are our alternatives: make an (irrational) leap into a circle of reasoning which is then seen to be reasonable (i.e., satisfying, though circular), or lapse into self-contradiction, which is neither reasonable nor unreasonable, but *blankness*. A self-contradiction is something we cannot think, whether reason works or not. What we cannot do we cannot do, and there's an end to it. We therefore cannot be epistemological sceptics or even agnostics. It is not merely unplausible or very hard to do: it is impossible to do, both physically and logically and in every other way if there be such. We may annihilate ourselves, but we cannot *be* sceptics. We reason to pull the trigger.

Again, if we reason we see many reasons for trusting it: if we pretend that we do not reason, it is only that we do not reason at "high" levels, for our *cells* reason on a low level while we live. But let us not forget the moral: that the whole thing is truly and hopelessly circular, if inevitable. To move at all it is necessary to exercise *trust,* to make a blind move of the will, thus showing the fundamental nature of such moves in general. After this first trusting step in the dark we gain sight, but only afterwards. But if the case is thus with the Cartesian circle, it is no less true with the examination of *any* hypothesis, particularly so with those of art or metaphysics. One has to open one's mind by an act of the will to the new insight and try to get a sympathetic feeling for it. Thus, on the question of God's existence, to take an extreme case, one has to believe first, or a least (and perhaps this latter is what the theologians have really meant) open one's mind very wide indeed, see the world from the perspective of this insight and see if it does not warm one's heart (i.e., appear reasonable).[8]

In summary, there are only two statements: (1) I believe in reason; (2) I do not believe in reason. If we say (2) we deceive ourselves, for with every breath we take we employ reason to a greater or lesser extent. But if we say (1), then we are empowered to say, "I know reason yields truth (or tends to)." True, the belief (the act of will) preceeds the knowledge (seeing reasons), but in all of us the belief is really there so the knowledge *may* be there if we examine the evidence. The reason so many sceptics have claimed to doubt that reason is truly reliable is probably to be found in the faulty view of proof that has prevailed in classical philosophy.

[8] Peirce very acutely points out that we only say things are "reasonable" when we cannot make a conclusive test on them but rather have to rely upon our sense of the fittingness of the situation.

C. CONCLUSIONS

If it is true, as we have been urging in various ways throughout this book, that volition, feeling, and logic are intermixed,[9] the foundations of all philosophical thought must be reconsidered, no matter how long that day of reckoning is postponed. In our day, analytic philosophy shies away from admitting such an intermixture, though it seems also occasionally to suspect its truth. The existential philosophy eagerly embraces the idea that will and feeling are involved in human reason. But representatives of this school so often philosophize from that insight in such an eccentric and in some cases adolescent fashion that for the most part they have failed to communicate with the larger philosophic community. In time, they will have to slow down and calm down and present their findings – albeit those findings are "against" reason – in a more reasonable style.

David Savan, in a delightful article,[10] "Decision and Knowledge in Peirce," argues, just as we have done, that for Peirce, man's volitional and aesthetic natures are so bound up in his mental life that it becomes nonsense to speak of "pure reason" apart from man's goals and hopes, his self-control and his values. This, Savan says, makes Peirce an existentialist. He adds that of course neither Peirce's style, temper, nor spirit could be thus described.[11] Surely by now we are not shocked to hear William James spoken of in such terms, that is, as a kind of prope-existentialist. And F. C. S. Schiller even more clearly merits such a description. But to hear Peirce so described is a jarring experience, but wholesome.

Much of the English speaking philosophical world has stubbornly closed itself up against this line of thought – that is, the relationship between reason and will – and has tended to bury its head in the sand of an alleged "pure logic" or "pure analysis." It has desperately hoped to keep philosophy unadulterated. It has aimed to keep the mind unspotted from the worlds of will and sentiment, sensing, no doubt correctly, that the classic English positivism, nominalism, and atomism, which all of us love from deep in our philosophic hearts, are thus doomed. It is no news to say that English philosophy has always been far from life, far from the lives of the philosophers themselves, as Hume so ingenuously admitted. But if we must abandon our pet ways of doing philosophy, the jolt we ex-

---

[9] For a further discussion on this subject see our chapter "The Relation between the Will, the Reason, and the Good," in *The Freewill Question* (The Hague: Martinus Nijhoff, 1971).

[10] *Transactions of the Charles S. Peirce Society*, Vol. 1, No. 2, Fall 1965, pp. 35ff.

[11] *Ibid.*, p. 50.

perience will be a growing and maturing pain. When we trouble ourselves to examine human life and destiny from these wider perspectives
opened up for us by these classic American philosophers, we may for our
trouble be rewarded with a vastly more hopeful and humane philosophy
than "pure reason," itself of course only a fiction, ever afforded.

WORKS CITED

(For a complete bibliography see note following)

Aquinas, Thomas. *On Being and Essence*. Armand Maurer, translator. Toronto: The Pontifical Institute of Medieval Studies, 1949.
Berkeley, George. "Criticism of Newton's Doctrine of Space," *Philosophy of Science*. Arthur Danto and Sidney Morgenbesser, (edd.). New York: The World Publishing Co., 1960.
Bernstein, Richard J. (ed.) *Perspectives on Peirce*. New Haven: Yale University Press, 1965.
Blanshard, Brand. *The Nature of Thought*. London, 1939.
Boler, John F. *Charles Peirce and Scholastic Realism*. Seattle: University of Washington Press, 1963.
Buchler, Justus. *Charles Peirce's Empiricism*. London: Kegan Paul, Trench, Trubner & Co. Ltd., 1939.
—. (ed.) *The Philosophy of Peirce*. New York: Harcourt, Brace & Co., 1940.
Cheng, Chung-Ying. "Charles Peirce's Arguments for the Nonprobabilistic Validity of Induction." *Transactions of the Charles S. Peirce Society*. III, 1 (Spring 1967), 24-39.
—. *Peirce's and Lewis's Theories of Induction*. The Hague: Martinus Nijhoff, 1969.
Davis, William H. *The Freewill Question*. The Hague: Martinus Nijhoff, 1971.
Descartes, René. "Discourse on Method." *The European Philosophers From Descartes to Nietzsche*, Monroe C. Beardsley (ed.) New York: The Modern Library, 1969.
Ewing, A. C. *The Fundamental Questions of Philosophy*. London: Routledge & Kegan Paul, Ltd., 1951.
Feibleman, James. *An Introduction to Peirce's Philosophy*. New York: Harper & Bros. Pub., 1948.
Fisch, Max H. (ed.) *Classic American Philosophers*. New York: Appleton-Century-Crofts, Inc., 1951.
Fitzgerald, John J. "Peirce's Theory of Inquiry." *Transactions of the Charles S. Peirce Society*. IV, 3 (Fall 1968), 130-143.
—. *Peirce's Theory of Signs as Foundation for Pragmatism*. The Hague: Mouton & Co., 1966.
Gallie, H. B. *Peirce and Pragmatism*. Middlesex: Penguin Books, 1952.
Goodman, Nelson. *The Structure of Appearnace*. Cambridge: Harvard University Press, 1951.

Goudge, Thomas A. *The Thought of C. S. Peirce*. Toronto: The University of Toronto Press, 1950.

Haas, William Paul, O. P. *The Conception of Law and the Unity of Peirce's Philosophy*. Notre Dame: The University of Notre Dame Press, 1964.

Hanson, Norwood Russell. *Patterns of Discovery*. Cambridge: At the University Press, 1958.

Hume, David. "An Enquiry Concerning Human Understanding." *The English Philosophers From Bacon to Hume*. Edwin A. Burtt (ed.). New York: The Modern Library, 1939.

—. *A Treatise of Human Nature*. L. A. Selby-Bigge, (ed.) Oxford: At the Clarendon Press, 1888.

James, William. *Pragmatism*. New York: The World Pub. Co., 1955.

Kant, Immanuel. *Critique of Pure Reason*. Norman Kemp Smith, translator. New York: Macmillan & Co., 1961.

Knight, Thomas. *Charles Peirce*. New York: Washington Square Press, 1965.

Koestler, Arthur. *The Act of Creation*. New York: Dell Publishing Co., 1964.

Körner, S. *The Philosophy of Mathematics*. London: Hutchinson & Co., 1960.

Land, Edwin H. "Experiments in Color Vision." *Scientific American*. CC (May 1959), 84-99.

Lewis, C. S. *The Abolition of Man*. New York: The Macmillan Co., 1953.

Lovejoy, Arthur O. "What Is the Pragmaticist Theory of Meaning? The First Phase." See under Wiener, Philip P.

Miller, Dickinson S. "Professor Donald Williams versus Hume" *The Journal of Philosophy*. XLIV, 25 (December 1947), 673-684.

Murphey, Murray G. *The Development of Peirce's Philosophy*. Cambridge: Harvard University Press, 1961.

"Kant's Children: The Cambridge Pragmatists." *Transactions of the Charles S. Peirce Society*. IV, 1 (Winter 1968), 13.

Nagel, Ernest and Newman, James R., "Goedel's Proof," *The World of Mathematics*, James R. Newman (ed.), III. New York: Simon & Schuster, 1956.

Newton, Isaac. "Absolute and Relative Space, Time, and Motion." See under George Berkeley.

Pap, Arthur. *An Introduction to the Philosophy of Science*. New York: The Free Press of Glencoe, 1962.

Pascal, Blaise. *Pensees*. William F. Trotter (trans.) New York: Washington Square Press, 1965.

Peirce, Charles Sanders. *Collected Papers*. Charles Harshorne and Paul Weiss, (edd.). Cambridge: The Belknap Press of Harvard University Press, 1960. Volumes one through six.

—. *Collected Papers*. Volumes seven and eight. Arthur W. Burks, (ed.). Cambridge: The Belknap Press of Harvard University Press, 1966.

Pinkham, Gordon N. "Some Comments on Cheng, Peirce, and Inductive Validity." *Transactions of the Charles S. Peirce Society*. III, 2 (Fall 1967), 96-107.

Poincaré, Henri. "Mathematical Creation," *The Creative Process*. Brewster Chiselin, (ed.) New York: The New American Library, 1952.

Quine, Willard V. O. *From a Logical Point of View*. Cambridge: Harvard University Press, 1953.

Reichenbach, Hans. *The Rise of Scientific Philosophy*. Berkeley: The University of California Press, 1966.

Russell, Bertrand. *A History of Western Philosophy*. New York: Simon & Schuster, 1945.

—. "non-Demonstrative Inference and Induction." *The Structure of Scientific Thought*. Edward H. Madden (ed.) Boston: Houghton Mifflin Co., 1960.

—. *Sceptical Essays*. London: George Allen & Unwin, Ltd., 1938.

Savan, David. "Decision and Knowledge in Peirce," *Transactions of the Charles S. Peirce Society*, I, 2 (Fall 1965).

Smullyan, Arthur F. "Implications of Critical Common-Sensism," See under Wiener, Philip P.

Spinoza, Benedict. "On the Improvement of the Understanding," *Spinoza Selections*, John Wild (ed.) New York: Charles Scribner's Sons, 1930.

Thompson, Manley. *The Pragmatic Philosophy of C. S. Peirce*. Chicago: The University of Chicago Press, 1953.

Waismann, Friedrich. "Language Strata," *Logic and Lauguage*, Antony Flew (ed.) New York: Doubleday & Co., 1965.

Weiss, Paul. "The Logic of the Creative Process." See under Weiner, Philip P.

Wells, Rulon. "Peirce as an American." See under Bernstein, Richard J.

Wennerberg, Hjalmar. *The Pragmatism of C. S. Peirce*. Copenhagen: Bjnar Munksgaard, 1962.

Whitehead, Alfred North. *Process and Reality*. New York: Harper & Bros., 1929.

—. *Science and the Modern World*. New York: The New American Library, 1948.

Wiener, Philip P. and Young, Frederic H. (edd.) *Studies in the Philosophy of Charles Sanders Peirce*. Cambridge: Harvard University Press, 1952.

Williams, Donald C. *The Ground of Induction*. New York: Russell & Russell, 1947.

Wisdom, John. *Paradox and Discovery*. Berkeley: The University of California Press, 1969.

—. *Philosophy and Psychoanalysis*. Berkeley: The University of California Press, 1969.

Further Bibliographical Information

There is a wealth of new material about Peirce appearing yearly, even monthly. The nearest thing to a complete bibliography may be obtained by combining the following sources: (1) Peirce's works; (a) Arthur W. Burk, *Bibliography of the Works of Charles Sanders Peirce* in Vol. VIII of *Collected Papers*, pp. 249-330. (b) "A First Supplement" in *Studies in the Philosophy of Charles Sanders Peirce, Second Series* Edward C. Moore and Richard S. Robin (edd.), (Univ. of Mass. Press, 1964), pp. 477-485. (c) "A Second Supplement," Max H. Fisch, *Transaction's of the Charles S. Peirce Society*, II, 1 (Spring 1966), pp. 51-53. (2) Works about Peirce; (a) "A Draft of a Bibliography of Writings about C. S. Peirce," in Moore and Robin, *op. cit.*, pp. 486-514 (b) "A First Supplement to 'A Draft of a Bibliography of Writings about C. S. Peirce,'" Max H. Fisch, *Transactions of the Charles S. Peirce Society*, II, 1 (Spring 1966), pp. 54-59.

INDEX

abduction, 2, 4, 22-27, 110f, 114, 143ff
absolute motion, 59
agapasticism (see love)
American philosophy, 5
analytic, 7
anthropomorphism, 130f
Aquinas, 97
Aristotle, 1, 15, 16
Association, law of, 2, 7, 32, 143
atomism, 11
automatic control, 65
axioms, 3, 7

Beardsley, M. C., 103
Beethovan, 127
behaviorism, 17f
belief, 103, 153ff
Bentham, 93
Bergson, 141
Berkeley, 7, 59f, 92f, 102, 104f
black box, 34f, 43
blank tablet, 123
Blanshard, B., 112
blind spot, 9
Boler, J. F., 48f
Boodha, 70
Boswell, 70, 112
Buchler, J., 13, 18, 25, 51, 73, 77, 81, 102, 105, 114, 120, 133
Burtt, E. A., 62, 132

cash value, 75, 88f
Catholics, 58
centrifugal force, 59
Chadwick, J., 111
chance, 121f
chemistry, 58

Cheng, Chung-Ying, 41f
Christ, 58
circularity, 20, 32, 37, 108f, 146-156
circular motion, 59
color vision, 9
common sense, 67, 108f, 121-133
computer, 17
Comte, 55
conceive, 51f, 78
Confucius, 70
conservatism, 137ff
consistency, 17, 27
continuity (see synechism)
Copernicus, 119
Copi, I. M., 111
correspondence theory, 79
creativity, 26
cryptography, 111

Danto, A., 59
Davis, W. H., 155
deduction, 2f, 21, 98f
Descartes, 1, 3, 5-21, 101, 103f, 109, 114f, 132, 142, 147, 153
Dewey, J., 5, 51, 124
diminsionality, 9f
dogmatism, 65
dream, 8

Einstein, A., 2, 44, 60
emotions, 13, 15
empiricism, 6, 78f, 89, 94
Eucharist, 58
Euclid, 7, 26, 97, 99f
evolution, 121f
Ewing, A. C., 33
existentialism, 155f
experience, 69